WORKING WHILE AUTISTIC

Thrive in a Career You Love

Wendela Whitcomb Marsh, MA, RSD

WORKING WHILE AUTISTIC
Thrive in a Career You Love

All marketing and publishing rights guaranteed to and reserved by:

FUTURE HORIZONS
(817) 277-0727
www.fhautism.com

© 2025 Wendela Whitcomb Marsh
All rights reserved.

Cover and interior by John Yacio III.

No part of this product may be reproduced in any manner whatsoever without written permission of Future Horizons, Inc., except in the case of brief quotations embodied in reviews or unless noted within the book.

ISBN: 978-1-963367-19-5

This book is for
autistic employees, employers, and mentors;
those who hold jobs they love;
those who seek employment better suited to their needs;
and those who have not yet entered the workforce.
You are worthy of your place.

Like everything I write and do, this book is also for
Cat David Robinson Marsh
Siobhan Eleanor Wise Marsh
Noel Maebh Whitcomb Marsh

and the dear memory of
David Scott Marsh.

CONTENTS

PART I: Ready to Work.................1

Chapter 1: Employability.....................3
Six Characters in Search of Employment 5
Messages from Autistic Mentors....................7

Chapter 2: Job Skills.......................9
SPACE 9
Six Characters in Search of Employment 17
Messages from Autistic Mentors...................28

Chapter 3: Job Search......................31
VIP 32
NOW 34
JACK..36
Six Characters in Search of Employment 39
Messages from Autistic Mentors...................47

Chapter 4: Interview.......................49
The 5 Ps to Be 50
Six Characters in Search of Employment 58
Messages from Autistic Mentors...................66

PART II: On the Job..........67

Chapter 5: You're Hired!..........69
Be Punctual..........70
Be Professional..........72
Be Prepared..........72
Be Positive..........73
Six Characters in Search of Employment..........74
Messages from Autistic Mentors..........84

Chapter 6: Work Ethic..........85
HERD CATS..........86
Six Characters in Search of Employment..........94
Messages from Autistic Mentors..........103

Chapter 7: Your Rights..........105
Should You Disclose Your Disability?..........106
How Much Should You Disclose?..........108
Who Should You Tell?..........109
What Are Reasonable Accommodations?..........109
Know Your Rights, but Avoid Fights..........110
CUPS..........111
Six Characters in Search of Employment..........113
Messages from Autistic Mentors..........127

Chapter 8: Your Kryptonite..........131
KRYPTONITE..........132

CONTENTS

Six Characters in Search of Employment 138
Messages from Autistic Mentors. .149

PART III: Pivot 151

Chapter 9: You're Fired! 153
BS 155
ER. 157
TRY. 158
Six Characters in Search of Employment 160
Messages from Autistic Mentors. .173

Chapter 10: I Quit! 175
ISSUES. 176
QUIT 180
Six Characters in Search of Employment 183
Messages from Autistic Mentors. .193

Chapter 11: Side Hustles 195
HUSTLE 196
Six Characters in Search of Employment 202
Messages from Autistic Mentors. .213

PART IV: Retirement and Beyond! 215

Chapter 12: Retirement Planning 217
SILVER. 219

Working While Autistic

    Six Characters in Search of Employment 221
    Messages from Autistic Mentors. 230

Chapter 13: The Adventure Continues **233**
    Six Characters Live and Work Happily Ever After. 233
    Messages from Autistic Mentors. 239
    Getting in the Last Word 239

IN GRATITUDE **243**

RESOURCES **245**

— PART I —
Ready to Work

"You can't get there by bus, only by hard work and risk and by not quite knowing what you are doing. What you'll discover will be wonderful. What you'll discover is yourself."
— *Alan Alda, actor* —

"I'm ready!"
— *SpongeBob SquarePants* —

– CHAPTER 1 –
Employability

"It is generally accepted that the happiest autistic adults work in their area of special interest ... Follow your passion always and maintain positive intent to serve humanity."

— *Philip Wylie*

Employment can be a major challenge for many autistic adults. Statistics suggest that anywhere between 66 percent and 85 percent of autistic adults are unemployed. Many more are underemployed and accept positions far below their education and ability. And yet, many autistic adults are highly skilled, motivated, and eager to work. They seem eminently employable. Why, then, is it so difficult?

Often, autistic adults mask hard (pretending to be "normal") to make it through the interview. They make a good first impression in the quiet interview room, for a limited space of time, where the expectations of asking and answering questions are clear. Unfortunately, the ability to maintain that same level of engagement

Working While Autistic

on a daily basis can be too much. Many workplaces are sensory and social nightmares, with changeable or unstructured schedules, unclear instructions, little to no feedback, and multiple interruptions. It's too much. Autists may unintentionally become "serial employees"; they get hired easily, but with each new job, they are either fired or they quit to save their own health.

Others don't have the capacity to mask sufficiently to get past the interview stage and show what they're really capable of. It's unfortunate that employers miss out by hiring the applicant who does the best job of interviewing, rather than the one who might be best at the actual job.

Are you aware of when you're masking and when and how to unmask? Sarah Teresa Cook, autistic writer, mentor, and facilitator, writes, "Brave noticing is the work of learning to trust your inspirations and creative impulses, of no longer trying to stuff them into the premade shapes so many of us inherited (and without consent) somewhere along the way." Are you bravely noticing your own masking? Doing so can allow you to choose it, or choose to unmask and honor your own needs. If you're new to unmasking (or even if you're not), I highly recommend Devon Price's book, *Unmasking Autism: Discovering the New Faces of Neurodiversity*. Price writes, "Refusing to perform neurotypicality is a revolutionary act of disability justice. It's also a radical act of self-love." You deserve radical self-love in your life and in your work.

In this book, we'll take a closer look at the hurdles involved in readiness to work and how to find and keep your ideal job. You'll find strategies, with examples of how these might play

– Chapter 1 –

out in fictional stories that feature Six Characters in Search of Employment. Each chapter closes with words of encouragement and hope shared by actually autistic people in "Messages from Autistic Mentors."

Are you ready? Let the adventure begin!

SIX CHARACTERS IN SEARCH OF EMPLOYMENT

DAISY

We first met Daisy as an autistic high school senior in *Independent Living While Autistic*, the first book in the *Adulting While Autistic* series. Later, we followed her relationship with Crow in *Relating While Autistic*, and finally, their unexpected parenting journey in *Parenting While Autistic*. Daisy still carries on internal dialogues with her Narrator, in conversations steeped in the lore of Dungeons & Dragons. We'll follow her employment journey from high school all the way through her path to retirement.

ZACH

Zach was a thirty-three-year-old autistic man who was anxious to finally get out of his parents' home and into the world of adulting in *Independent Living While Autistic*. We'll find out more about his employment journey here.

Working While Autistic

TRISH

We met Trish in *Dating While Autistic* when she and Bill had their first date. She was astonished to learn that Bill was autistic too. The romance continued, and she fell in love with Bill in *Relating While Autistic*. We followed their family's journey in *Parenting While Autistic*, but we never heard much about her career. In this book, we'll go back and find out how Trish got started in a career she loved.

BILL

Bill liked Trish as soon as they met in *Dating While Autistic*, and their friendship blossomed slowly into romance. They finally moved in together and married in *Relating While Autistic* and had a family together in *Parenting While Autistic*. Now we can go back in time and fill in Bill's work history, career challenges, and triumphs as he finds his comfort zone in the world of work.

MARIA

When we met Maria in *Independent Living While Autistic*, she was a divorced mother of twin girls who were in college when she realized that she was autistic. We learned more about her parenting journey in *Parenting While Autistic*. Maria never thought she'd be able to hold down a real job of her own, as she had always relied on her parents or her ex-husband to support her. We'll go more deeply into her employment path in this book.

– Chapter 1 –

ROBERT

When we met Robert in *Independent Living While Autistic*, he was a retired television repairman and a grandfather. He discovered he was autistic after his grandson was diagnosed. We learned more about his intergenerational grandparenting journey in *Parenting While Autistic*. In this book, we'll look more closely at his entire career path.

MESSAGES FROM AUTISTIC MENTORS

"I love being a drive-through greeter at the Starbucks window. If you like coffee and want to work at a Starbucks, the best place is the window because you get fresh air and you're separated from the noise of the blenders and coffee grinders. The customers are not there long enough for a long, drawn-out conversation, and you can script it."

— Suzanne, Starbucks drive-through window greeter

"It may not be for everyone, but I enjoy working with autistic children who have higher support needs. It helps me feel a lot less isolated in the world, like I can provide a bridge to them. It also gives me ways to learn about myself. I relate to the children I work with more than I relate to my colleagues. This job is a kindness I give to myself. It's changed my experience and my relationship with work. It is fulfilling, as well as keeping me from starving.

Working While Autistic

Before, I was trying to perform and keep my head above water. Now, having relevance to myself in my work, it is so much better. It brings me connection and trust, and I feel I'm doing something meaningful."

— Helena, autistic woman, works with autistic students

"I didn't know who I was when I first started working; I didn't know I was autistic or had PTSD, but I was drawn to work in the creative arts, theater, and writing. I did not try to become tenured or an administrator, which turned out to be a good choice for me."

— Beth F. Watzke, late-diagnosed autistic writer and animal care provider

– CHAPTER 2 –
Job Skills

Everybody Wants Someone with Skills

"People with highly transferable skills may be specialists in certain areas, but they're also incredible generalists—something businesses that want to grow need."

— *Leah Busque, entrepreneur and founder of TaskRabbit*

If you want a career you love, you'll need to develop the right skills for the job. Think SPACE: *self skills, people skills, authority skills, communication skills,* and *employment skills*. Master these to be on the right path.

SPACE

Self Skills

The S in SPACE stands for *self skills*.

The self skills you'll need to succeed include self-awareness, self-presentation, and self-control.

Working While Autistic

Self-Awareness

When you have self-awareness, you think about yourself and how others see you. At home, you might do your best thinking if you lean back and prop your feet up on the desk. If you sit the same way at work, people might think you're lazy or disrespectful. One of Temple Grandin's and Sean Barron's ten unwritten rules of social relationships is "People Act Differently in Public than They Do in Private." People with self-awareness skills know the difference and act accordingly.

You can develop your self-awareness skills. Consciously ask yourself what other people might think about you based on what you do or say. What kind of a first impression do you make? Do you send signals to show you're open to conversation, or is your body turned away? If you slouch with your head down and your arms crossed, you might ward people off. This can be useful with strangers on public transportation, but the same posture at work looks uncommunicative, like you're not a team player. Become more aware of yourself and how others see you; it's an important skill to develop.

Self-Presentation

Self-presentation is crucial. If you, your clothes, or your hair are unkempt, it won't matter if you're good at your job. Nobody wants to work next to someone who smells or has hair like a greasy rat's nest. Even though it doesn't make sense, when you have good hygiene, people are more open to what you have to say. You might think, "They should listen to me because I'm smart and have great

Chapter 2

ideas." Ideally, yes, but in reality, people seldom respect someone who looks or smells dirty. It's great to have a personal style, like always wearing a hair bow, or suspenders and a bow tie. Be aware, though, that if your style is too extreme, it might put people off. Examples would be wearing clothing that makes political statements, or that looks too much like a costume rather than work apparel.

One way you can develop self-presentation skills is to notice how coworkers present themselves. Model your own presentation on those around you. If there's a range of styles from blue jeans to suits, don't go straight to the most casual look. Dress for the job you want and consider a presentation that is slightly above, but not too high above, your current job. If your coworkers in the mail room wear jeans and your supervisor wears slacks and a buttoned shirt, don't wear a suit and tie. You might want to dress like the others at your level, or like the person just one step above you in the chain of command, but not like the CEO. That doesn't mean you can't be comfortable or have your own unique style, but if you want to develop your self-presentation skills, try to avoid extreme styles at work.

Self-Control

Self-control may be the most important self skill of all in the workplace. If you raise your voice or argue when your supervisor corrects you, it shows a lack of self-control. If you melt down, cry, or leave work when something unexpected happens, you could be reprimanded. If you lose your temper easily and fail to control

Working While Autistic

yourself, an angry outburst could get you fired. Someone who can't function under stress will not be seen as a valuable worker. The risks are too great for most companies to keep an employee who is seen as out of control.

If lack of self-control has been a major problem in your life, seek help. Talk to your doctor. A counselor or anger management coach can help. If you don't have a serious problem and you feel you can manage it yourself, check out *Independent Living While Autistic: Your Roadmap to Success*, in the chapter on self-management. It can help you create your own plan.

People Skills

The P in SPACE stands for *people skills*.

In addition to self skills, good people skills are vital in any career. Getting along with colleagues and customers will help you get and keep a job. This includes common courtesy and tact. If you pride yourself on your brutal honesty, learn to be truthful without being brutal. For instance, if a coworker shows you an ugly picture of their baby, be kind. Remember, *precious* means "of great value," and *adorable* means "able to be adored." A baby doesn't have to be cute to be called precious or adorable. Keep negative thoughts to yourself; it's an excellent people skill.

Never comment on anyone's body. Even a compliment about a woman's pretty blouse calls attention to her chest area, which is inappropriate. It's best to avoid giving compliments at the workplace. If you want to give an occasional compliment, stick to a person's talents and abilities, not their physical attributes. Beware

Chapter 2

if someone asks, "Do these pants make my behind look fat?" Under no circumstances should you say, "Of course not. It's your behind that makes the pants look fat." Funny does not excuse rudeness. Try a noncommittal response, such as, "You always look fine," then return the topic to work. Your coworkers should not be asking questions about their own appearance, but it's not your place to correct them. Just move on.

Put yourself in someone else's shoes to see their perspective. You can practice while you watch TV: Try to imagine what each character is thinking. What's their motivation? Do their words match their feelings? Are there any underlying nonverbal cues? Practice improves your people skills.

Authority Skills

The A in SPACE stands for *authority skills*.

Unless you're self-employed and have no supervisors or customers, you need to respond respectfully to authority figures. Some people find it difficult to work with a supervisor who's not as smart as they are. If you're highly intelligent, it'll be difficult to find a job where the boss is clearly your intellectual superior. Even so, it's not a good idea to let people know that you're smarter than they are. Don't patronize or imply that they won't understand you. Don't use big, pretentious words, but don't talk down to people either. You may have groups of friends who regularly speak in scientific terminology or very proper, formal English, and others who may speak and text in shorthand with no punctuation required. You may choose to modify your

Working While Autistic

language to match those you are with, although in social settings you are not required to mask your communication style for the benefit of others. In the workplace, it can be different. You don't want to give people at work the idea that you think you're better than they are, even if you do feel that way. Be respectful, always. If a supervisor says something you know to be wrong, do not call them out in front of others. If it's important, speak to them privately later. If it's minor, like saying, "Around the beginning of the month ..." don't correct them with, "Actually, it was on the twelfth of the month." Nit-picking will make you look like a jerk, and you're not a jerk. Knowing when to keep your opinions to yourself is an important skill, especially when dealing with those in authority.

This is a vital skill in all of life, not just at work, but also if you must interact with law enforcement. Be mindful of how they may perceive your attitude. Some people seem to believe that nonverbal expressions of exasperation or contempt are not real communication and that they should be judged on their words alone, but this is not the case. If you sigh heavily, roll your eyes, and use a sarcastic tone of voice with someone in authority, you will be judged harshly. Learn to curb these signals. When you show respect, you're more likely to be respected.

Communication Skills

The C in SPACE stands for *communication skills*.

In their book *Autism and Employment*, Lisa Tew and Diane Zajac wrote, "Strong social-communication skills help individuals

— Chapter 2 —

to interact productively and positively with others for any job." All communication has a social component; it doesn't happen in a vacuum. Good verbal and nonverbal skills are necessary. If your boss gives you a project and you walk away with no reply and no approximation of eye contact, they may assume you've ignored them or that you refuse to accept the assignment. Sure, you had a thousand brilliant ideas pop into your head as you walked silently away, but that won't matter if you get fired before you even start. Here are some tips for how to communicate when your boss gives you an assignment:

- First, make (or fake) eye contact. You don't have to actually look at their eyeballs if you dislike that, but do orient yourself toward them and look toward their face.
- Second, reflect back on what you think they said, such as, "I see, you want me to (summarize assignment), and you need it by (due date). Is that right?" Understand their expectations.
- Third, let them know that you'll get right to work on it. This is also the time to share your excitement if you think it's a great project, and/or to let them know if you might need support to get it done.
- Fourth, when you get back to your desk, send an email with a recap of the conversation so you'll have a written record to remind you of your new assignment, and to confirm that you understand. Let them know in the email that you're excited to start on the new project. This is not the time to make general negative or pessimistic remarks; give the project a chance. If you encounter problems, present them

Working While Autistic

along with possible solutions. Don't badmouth the project without offering strategies to make it better.

One of the most difficult types of communication at work is when the boss gives you constructive criticism. This can be hard to take, but it's important to accept it well. Put yourself in your employer's shoes. Would you rather have a worker who listens and tries to improve, or one who's stubborn, argumentative, and can't take correction? Be the one who accepts criticism graciously, and you'll make your boss's job easier.

Employment Skills

The E in SPACE stands for *employment skills*.

The employment skills you need depend on the job you want. Whatever the field, it's up to you to get those skills. Some careers require a high school diploma, or a college degree, or special training. Check out colleges, adult education courses, and online courses. Don't invest in a school unless you're sure it's reputable. Be smart and check your options before you commit.

Another way to get employment skills is to volunteer or intern in your field. You'll not only gain valuable experience for your resumé, but there's also a chance you may be offered a job. There's no guarantee, but it lets the employer see first-hand what kind of an employee you'd be. If you do an exemplary job and have a positive attitude and strong work ethic, you might get hired.

Not all of your skills may be marketable. Some may be difficult to monetize. Everyone wants a job testing video games or writing comic books, but those jobs are rare. Your personal passion may be

– Chapter 2 –

better used as a side hustle for extra pocket money while you keep your day job for a steady income and, hopefully, benefits. Even if your hobby does not bring you money, you should continue to pursue the things you love. The value of an interest or passion is unrelated to a potential paycheck.

Whatever your dream career is, learn the skills and get the training you need.

Now that we've explored SPACE, read how our six characters worked on their job skills.

SIX CHARACTERS IN SEARCH OF EMPLOYMENT

DAISY

DAISY: *(interrupts Mr. Hodge, English teacher)* Excuse me, you made a mistake grading my paper.

MR. HODGE: Be quiet, Daisy. I didn't call on you to speak.

DAISY: I know, because I didn't raise my hand. I just wanted to point out your mistake—

MR. HODGE: In this classroom, we raise our hands and wait to be called on before speaking out.

DAISY: Actually, no, "we" don't. You never raise your hand.

Working While Autistic

NARRATOR: *Our hero realizes she'd better talk fast so as to get her ideas out before Mr. Hodge interrupts her again. Fortunately, talking fast is one of her superpowers.*

DAISY: *(stands up and speaks quickly with no pauses)* You marked this wrong when I used "they" as a singular, and you wrote that it has to be plural, but that's incorrect because "they" can be singular for nongendered people.

MR. HODGE: People are not non-gendered, and "they" is plural. End of discussion. Now if you will kindly sit down, we can return to our lesson.

DAISY: But you're wrong. You're a teacher, and you're teaching everyone wrong things. How are we supposed to learn if the teachers are ignorant?

NARRATOR: *And so, our hero finds herself once more in a chair in the hallway, waiting to be called into the principal's office. To be punished when one is correct, that is an epic tragedy. If only Euripides or Shakespeare were here today, they could write the sad tale of Daisy, unjustly accused, whose only crime was speaking the truth.*

MR. CRAFT: Come in, Daisy. Have a seat.

– Chapter 2 –

DAISY: I don't know what Mr. Hodge told you, but I am being punished wrongfully for speaking the truth.

MR. CRAFT: It's not a question of whether what you said was true. The bottom line is you interrupted Mr. Hodge, corrected him in front of the whole class, refused to be quiet and sit down when asked, and publicly accused your teacher of ignorance.

DAISY: Well, when you say it like that, it sounds kind of bad.

MR. CRAFT: It is bad.

DAISY: But I was right!

MR. CRAFT: That's not going to be much of a comfort when you're suspended. This is your senior year, and English is required. You need to pass this class to graduate.

DAISY: He can't suspend me for being right!

MR. CRAFT: A teacher can suspend any student from *their* class—

DAISY: You just did it yourself, so I know I'm right.

MR. CRAFT: Did what?

Working While Autistic

DAISY: You said, "A teacher can suspend any student from *their* class." You used "their" to refer to a singular teacher, not plural teachers.

MR. CRAFT: When you focus on one detail like that, you miss the big picture. You, Daisy, have been suspended from Mr. Hodge's class for the rest of class today and all day tomorrow. You will not return to class, and tomorrow you will report to the vice principal fourth period and do your English assignment independently.

DAISY: But you proved I'm right in your own statement, so you can force Mr. Hodge to take it back because he was wrong.

MR. CRAFT: He was right that you interrupted him, he was right that you called him out disrespectfully in class, he was right that you failed to comply with his direction, and he was right that you insulted him publicly. Whether he was right or wrong about "they" is unimportant.

DAISY: But it's important to me!

MR. CRAFT: You have an opportunity to learn something about your own behavior here, Daisy, and if you're as smart as I think you are, you'll figure it out.

– Chapter 2 –

NARRATOR: *Daisy slumps and looks at the floor. What had she done that was so wrong? What could she have done differently?*

DAISY: Okay, the first thing, interrupting. I know I do that a lot. I always have. Usually, my mom or teachers put up with it because they like what I have to say. But not today.

MR. CRAFT: That is an understatement.

DAISY: So I guess if I notice a teacher says or does something incredibly stupid and witless and ignorant and—

MR. CRAFT: Moving along ...

DAISY: Right. So if I notice an error, I should keep it to myself? What if it's important to set the record straight, so all the other students don't learn something idiotic?

MR. CRAFT: If you felt it was important enough, how could you let a teacher know without calling them out in front of the whole class?

DAISY: Well, I guess I could write them a note later?

MR. CRAFT: You could.

Working While Autistic

DAISY: I never thought about him being embarrassed in front of everyone. I thought only kids got embarrassed.

MR. CRAFT: Teachers are people, too, and they have feelings.

DAISY: Okay. And the other thing, when he asked me to sit down and shut up—

MR. CRAFT: Did he say shut up?

DAISY: Not in so many words, but that's what he was thinking, I could tell.

MR. CRAFT: Pay attention to what you're saying here, Daisy. There's something important.

DAISY: Hmm. So, he was really mad at me, wasn't he?

MR. CRAFT: Oh yes.

DAISY: But he didn't yell at me or tell me to shut up or call me names or anything.

MR. CRAFT: He did not. Because he is a professional, and he has self-control. You would be wise to learn some self-control, Daisy, especially around authority figures.

DAISY: What makes authority figures so special? They're human, too, no better than me.

– Chapter 2 –

MR. CRAFT: But people in authority have power. A teacher assigns grades. If a portion of your grade is related to classroom participation and he remembers your participation today, your grade could suffer.

DAISY: So I should just suck up to him because he's a teacher?

MR. CRAFT: You should control your impulse to make choices that are disrespectful of others and could harm you in the future. That's not the same as sucking up. If you were at work and your boss made a mistake and you called them out in front of everyone, they could fire you. In school, teachers are paid to teach all students, even if they're obnoxious, but once you graduate, it's a different world. No one has to put up with insults.

DAISY: I never thought about that. Is there something I should do so Mr. Hodge won't be so mad at me?

MR. CRAFT: You're an adult now. What do you think?

DAISY: I think I should write him a letter of apology. And tell him I won't act out like that in class again.

Working While Autistic

MR. CRAFT: I knew you were smart. I'll release you to go to the library for the rest of fourth period, and you can write your letter. Tomorrow you're on in-school suspension, but you can give him your letter the next day.

NARRATOR: *Daisy spends a lot of time in thought during her suspension. She isn't used to reining in her impulse to say exactly what she thinks as soon as it pops into her head. This is something she realizes she will need to work on. She hopes never to have a boss as ignorant as Mr. Hodge.*

ZACH

As he left the temple after the young adult group, Zach saw a new notice on the bulletin board. They were looking for someone part-time to do general caretaking: unlock buildings for various groups, lock up at night, and make rounds occasionally to check for litter and ensure everything was safe. Since Zach's parents lived nearby, it sounded like something he could easily do. He was already familiar with the various buildings and courtyard, so he wouldn't have to get used to a new place. But did he have the skills to do this job? He thought about it.

Zach knew he was physically able to make rounds and do basic caretaking tasks. Could he handle the responsibility though? It would be terrible if he forgot to lock up at night. Time awareness had not always been one of his skills, and he didn't want to blow

— Chapter 2 —

it at his first job by being forgetful. Then he thought about the smartphone his parents had given him for Hanukkah. It wasn't just for games and texting; he could set it to remind him to do what he needed to do. Zach decided that he did have what it took to apply for the job.

Zach unpinned the notice from the bulletin board and took it to the rabbi's office. He wanted to remember what it said. Then he thought that might look presumptuous, as if he thought he would definitely get the job, so they wouldn't need it on the board anymore. He hesitated outside the rabbi's open door and looked down at the notice in his hand, suddenly embarrassed.

"Can I help you with something, Zachary?" The rabbi looked at him quizzically, and he wondered how long he'd been there.

"I'm going to put this back," he said quickly.

"Oh?"

"I mean, as soon as I talk to you, I'll put it right back. I wasn't trying to steal it. I just wanted to remember what it said."

"Perhaps you could come in and tell me what we're talking about." The rabbi had a kind smile, and Zach came in and sat on the edge of the chair in front of the desk.

"I saw this job notice on the bulletin board, and I want to apply, but then I'll put it back so other people can see it too," he said. "I didn't mean to keep it."

"Understandable." Rabbi nodded. "So what does it say?"

Zach read the notice to the rabbi. The rabbi said he should pick up an application from the secretary and turn it in, and that he would put in a good word for him with the trustees.

Working While Autistic

"Thank you, Rabbi!" Zach jumped up. "I'll do that right now." He started to rush out, and then he turned back. "But first I'll go put this back on the bulletin board."

TRISH

Trish had a job she loved, one that she felt comfortable with. She worked in the admissions office of her alma mater. She had started as an intern when she was a student and was offered a full-time job after graduation. She had learned the skills she needed as a student, and they already knew her work, so it was a painless transition. She was always happiest in the back office, behind the scenes, where she could hide behind a computer and avoid people. Trish steadfastly resisted all offers of career advancement, because that would have meant traveling to high schools, and giving campus tours to visiting families. She was happiest working on the application paperwork and process, without meeting the actual students. She felt she knew them through the paper trails of letters from their teachers, extra-curricular activities, and personal essays. She cherished each of them with no need to meet face-to-face.

BILL

Bill had loved computers his whole life, so he was thrilled to get a job in the field that meant so much to him. During all the time he had spent "playing" with his computers and gadgets, as his parents believed, he was actually developing skills that would ensure his future professional security and happiness.

– Chapter 2 –

MARIA

Maria needed a job. She wouldn't get spousal support forever. Although her needs were simple and her overhead low, she needed an income of her own. The problem was, she hated the idea of working with other people. The thought of it made her anxious, so she turned on Sloth TV to relax. After she felt calmer, she asked the internet about jobs that could be done from home. There was telemarketing, but Maria hated talking on the phone. Finally, she found the ideal job for her: editing and proofreading from home. Maria thought she was perfect for this job: she had good attention to detail and extensive knowledge of the rules of good writing. She was often bothered by errors she saw in online posts and wished she could correct them. Shouldn't everyone know the difference between *your* and *you're*, or *there*, *their*, and *they're*? She would be happy to share her knowledge and get paid for it, all while working at home. But was she good enough to be a professional? She wasn't sure. Maria went online and took several free proofreading tests. She discovered that she was, indeed, very good at this. She had the skills, and now she would pay the bills ... at least, as soon as she found a job.

ROBERT

Time was not Robert's friend. There was too much of it since he retired. Often, he felt like he was wasting time, spinning his wheels, getting under his wife's feet. He missed having a job to go to. He loved his old job, repairing good old cathode-ray tube (CRT) television sets. Nowadays, though, everybody wanted

Working While Autistic

those flat-screen liquid crystal displays (LCDs) and would rather buy new than repair their old sets. How was he going to put his old-time skills to work in this day and age? He wasn't keen on learning a whole new technology, so he'd have to find someplace that valued the skills he already had. Robert guessed he had his work cut out for him, but he was ready to work, and up for the search.

MESSAGES FROM AUTISTIC MENTORS

"When I first started thinking about selling my art at conventions, I feared my work wasn't good enough. I also worried about the social aspect. Then I realized that most of the people at these cons share interests with me, or they wouldn't be there. They'd be glad to see artwork of their favorite characters, even if it wasn't perfect. Also, a lot of them are shy and have difficulty communicating, too, so I shouldn't worry so much. I learned that actively socializing and using aggressive sales tactics with potential customers (which I'm not comfortable with) actually harms sales. Being visible, standing behind the table, and using relaxed body language, on the other hand, benefits sales."

— Noel, autistic artist

"The best skills for a service job like drive-through window greeter are being able to follow a basic script and money-handling skills.

– Chapter 2 –

Even though the cash register tells you how much change is needed, you have to know different ways to make change quickly using the coins you have. Being able to communicate fairly well is also important."

— Suzanne, drive-through window greeter

"Skills are really important. Sometimes I'm quick to learn new things, or it might take me longer, but I try to give myself space and be honest with myself about the skills and training I need."

— Helena, works with autistic students

"Computer skills are important, and being able to relate to different people, groups, and communities."

— Beth F. Watzke, late-diagnosed autistic writer and animal care provider

– CHAPTER 3 –
Job Search
The Hunt Is On

"When it comes to actually looking for a job ... for autistic people ... instead of going out and searching for roles ... LinkedIn can make the roles come to you."

— *James Ward-Sinclair,* Autistic & Unapologetic

The first step on your road to employment, once you have the skills you need, is the job search. I've got some tips that will help you become a VIP NOW, JACK. Yes, I realize that sounds extremely silly, but if you know me at all, you know that I am not above it.

So let's begin.

VIP stands for *volunteer, intern, portfolio/resumé*.

NOW stands for *network, online search, work experience*.

JACK stands for *job fairs, alumni, cold calls, and know someone*.

Working While Autistic

VIP

Volunteer

The V in VIP stands for *volunteer*.

When you start your job search, you will meet challenges. Employers want someone with experience, but if they don't give you a job, how can you get experience? If you volunteer in your chosen field, this will give you the experience you need. If you haven't done any volunteer work yet, there's no time like the present. Get out there and volunteer. It will give you confidence as you learn to navigate workplaces. It will also give you something to put on your resumé. And who knows? You might meet someone who can give you a reference or help you get your foot in the door of your first paid job.

Intern

The I in VIP stands for *intern*.

If your chosen career field uses interns, this is a good place to start. Some internships are paid positions, and others are unpaid. It's great if you can get paid while you learn, but don't turn down an unpaid internship if it's offered and you don't have something better at the moment. Employers learn what kind of a worker you are during an internship, and sometimes they hire their new employees from the intern pool. This is the perfect opportunity to make a good impression, especially if you're not as good in interviews as you are on the job.

– Chapter 3 –

Portfolio/Resumé

The P in VIP stands for *portfolio or resumé*.

Applicants who are not comfortable in an interview can put the focus on what they have demonstrated they are capable of, rather than how well they chat with the interview panel. Create a portfolio of your work or a resumé that highlights your relevant experience. It's a great way to show, rather than tell, why they should hire you. When you start out, you shouldn't spend hundreds of dollars on a professional portfolio or resumé. You can do it yourself with free online tutorials. Alter it slightly to fit what each employer wants. You don't want a one-size-fits-all, cookie-cutter resumé that looks like every other one they receive. Personalize it, and keep it focused. Your encyclopedic knowledge of tropical fish might help you get a job in an aquarium or pet store, but not a furniture store. They should recognize that you are the right person for their job, not just any job. Once your portfolio or resumé is finished, show it to a trusted mentor or friend who understands your field, and ask for honest and supportive constructive feedback. Reread it, polish it, and make it shine. Once it's as good as you can make it, send it out to prospective employers.

Working While Autistic

NOW

Network

The N in NOW stands for *network*.

Networking can be cringey. No one wants to feel manipulated or used, or that you're only interested in what they can do for you. And you probably don't want to be pushy and shove your business card at everyone you meet. It feels forced and uncomfortable. Respect that feeling, and don't network in the traditional way of marketing yourself to everyone you meet. Not every elevator ride has to include a pitch. Be prepared with a short, rehearsed sentence or two about what you do or your chosen field, but don't pitch it unless someone asks for it. Maybe you have a box of business cards, or a scannable card that can send your information and QR code automatically to someone's phone. That's great, but don't tell everyone you meet about it (even though a scannable QR code business card sounds extremely cool). If they ask for your card, then you can bring it out or offer to scan your information to them. If they don't ask, you're not required to offer. It's so easy to come across as pushy, which is the last thing you want.

If you go to a business-related event where people are expected to mingle and network, it's okay to be a "wallflower" and talk to only a few people. You don't have to be a shark swimming through the room in search of potential prey. If you stay on the fringes and talk to two or three people who are also on the edges, that's fine. Think quality, not quantity. You can leave early and count it as a success. You did a difficult thing, and you should feel good about it.

– Chapter 3 –

Online Search

The O in NOW stands for *online search*.

Is online one of your favorite ways to connect with the world? If so, you are ready for this. When you search online for potential employment opportunities, keep your online searches positive and upbeat. Don't get bogged down by all the fascinating rabbit holes that will pop up to distract you. Stay focused. You don't have to use every form of social media; it won't all be consistent with your style. Many people use LinkedIn to look for jobs, or Facebook. You'll often find groups of others in your field that you can join. Like and follow people you admire and want to learn from. Share blogs or posts that you find inspiring or helpful. There might be discussions where you can ask for advice, but be sure to follow the rules of the group before you post. Many autistic people are far more comfortable and effective online than they are in person, so use that strength to your advantage. While you're researching job listings, have an open mind. You may think you are unqualified for a particular job in your field, but don't let that stop you. If you meet the minimum requirements, go ahead and apply even if you don't meet the employer's "wish list" of what they're looking for. Even if you don't get the job, you will have had more experience in applying and interviewing, and it may be that you are exactly the person they were looking for. They didn't know because they just hadn't met you yet.

Working While Autistic

Work Experience

The W in NOW stands for *work experience*.

If you're a student, find out about the work experience programs available at your school. Sign yourself up and get the most you can from what they have to offer. Even if they assign you a part-time job that is not in your chosen field, the experience you gain dealing with supervisors and coworkers will be helpful in any career. If you do a good job, be sure to ask your work experience employer and school contact person for letters of recommendation to add to your portfolio. If you're out of school, check out your state or county's vocational rehabilitation office for opportunities. Get an appointment with a vocational counselor to talk about your career goals and to see what kinds of work experiences they might offer. Ask about special services for people with disabilities. Their goal is to connect people with jobs that match their skills, abilities, and interests. Let them help you.

JACK

Job Fairs

The J in JACK stands for *job fairs*.

Job fairs, or career fairs, can be a great opportunity, but as with many opportunities, it has its pros and cons.

On the pro side, you can connect with many employers in one day, ask them questions, and learn about what their company has to offer. You can also meet them outside of an interview setting,

— Chapter 3 —

which may be more relaxed. This is a good opportunity to leave your resumé and business cards with many representatives; after all, that's what they're here for.

On the con side, there may be crowds of other job-seekers who all want to be seen and heard and make a good impression. If you don't do well in crowds, and if you dislike competition, especially with pushy people, you may not want to spend a lot of time there. However, if you at least show up, hand out a few resumés, and leave early if you need to for your own self-care, you will have taken a positive step.

Alumni

The A in JACK stands for *alumni*.

If you or anyone in your family went to the same school as the person who will interview you, especially if it's you and not your second cousin once removed, then mention the connection. You can usually find chief officers' alma maters on the company website. This one's a long shot, but if you do happen to connect over shared college experiences, it can help them remember you when they make their decisions.

Cold Calls

The C in JACK stands for *cold calls*.

This is the worst. Cold calls are no fun to receive or to make. Most of the time, avoid this one. Email exists for a reason. However, there may be a time when the best course of action is to pick up your phone and call, especially if they asked you to call them. If they asked, it's not really a cold call, is it? Most autistic people I know would rather not talk on the phone if they can avoid it. If you can't avoid it, plan a brief script of what you want to say, and write the bullet points so you can remember your ideas and won't have to read the script verbatim. That usually sounds stuffy or less than natural. Before the call, use whatever relaxation strategies work for you, such as mindful breathing, stretching, a short walk out in nature, or whatever helps you focus. Plan to do something you enjoy right after the call to celebrate that you did a difficult thing, however it turns out.

Know Someone

The K in JACK stands for *know someone*.

If you know someone in the career field of your dreams, that's wonderful! Ask them for any advice they can offer you, or if they know of openings that you might be a good fit for. Don't drop their names without their permission though. Gauge the closeness of your relationship before you approach them. You don't want to come across as a user who's only interested in what they can do for you. If the person you know is your parent, they might help you figure out who to approach and how. If the person you know is a good friend you see often, it's usually fine to ask them for help, too, within reason. For instance, have you helped them move, cared for their pets while they were on vacation, or driven them to the airport? If so, now is the time to ask them for a return favor. On the other hand, if the person you know is a distant relative or someone you knew in school that you don't regularly keep in touch

— Chapter 3 —

with, don't beg for favors. It's fine to ask for advice, but don't ask them to put in a good word with their boss for you. It's also fine to ask a previous boss to write you a letter of recommendation or to be on a list of references to be contacted. Get their permission before you put them on the list. If you didn't leave on good terms or the boss didn't even know your name, don't ask. If you had a supervisor who appreciated your work, do ask for a letter or for them to serve as a reference for you. It's not who you know, but who knows you and will speak of you highly.

SIX CHARACTERS IN SEARCH OF EMPLOYMENT

DAISY

NARRATOR: *Our hero, Peridot Goldhammer the Mighty (aka Daisy), strode confidently into the Work Experience classroom, ready to take on the world of work. Having completed six sessions on employability with Lucie the Life Coach, she was ready for anything.*

MR. WORTH: Welcome, everyone, please take a seat. I'm Mr. Worth, and I'll be your Work Experience teacher this semester. It's my goal to find gainful employment for each and every one of you before midterms.

Working While Autistic

DAISY: *(raises her hand)* Will we get to choose the job we want?

MR. WORTH: Well, we hope to find a good match for you, but we can't guarantee the perfect job right out of the gate.

NARRATOR: *Our hero wonders what this gate is and how powerful the gatekeeper might be. Her D&D experience may be helpful in vanquishing any opposition to her perfect job. She decides not to ask about the gate, however, as it is likely to be a mystical metaphor or stealthy synonym, the twin banes to her personal quest of conquering conversation.*

MR. WORTH: I'm passing out a questionnaire for you to complete. This will help us find the right job for you, among those available through the school. We'll do our best to get you in the door and to provide follow-up support.

NARRATOR: *Daisy reads and answers the questions:*

> What gets her up in the morning?
> *Coffee.*
>
> What helps her calm down when stressed?
> *Nature.*

— Chapter 3 —

NARRATOR:
(continued)

> What is her personal passion?
> *Dungeons & Dragons.*
>
> What is her work experience?
> *None, she's a high school student.*
>
> What kind of job would she like best?
> *Low stress, limited dealings with the public.*
>
> What kind of job would she like least?
> *Anything stressful or crowded or noisy.*

Our hero is encouraged by the kinds of questions that were asked. It reminds her of her work with Lucie the Life Coach. Her future in the world of work seems somehow less daunting, with a work experience program to help guide her through the labyrinth of employment.

ZACH

Even though he was excited about the possibility of working part-time at the temple as a caretaker, Zach knew that this would not be enough for him to make a living and afford to move out of his parents' house. He would continue his job search online.

Three things were helpful to Zach in his job search. The first one was when he changed his attitude from negative to positive. It started as simply as changing his online searches from "Why can't I get a job?" to "How can I get a job?" That shift made a difference

Working While Autistic

to his outlook. Even though it didn't suddenly open doors to him, he found that by not getting bogged down in other people's online complaints in the comments sections, he felt more optimistic when he read about what jobs were available, even when there weren't a lot to choose from.

Second, Zach had volunteered with a political party he supported, and this gave him a lot of excellent experience taking on and completing tasks, as well as interacting with coworkers. Even though he had no desire to go into politics as a career, he loved hanging out with people who agreed with him. Not only that, but he felt like he was making a positive difference in the world instead of complaining about what was wrong. Because he had shown that he could follow directions and be a productive team member, his supervisor offered to write him a letter of recommendation.

Finally, if Zach got this job at the temple, even though it wasn't his ultimate career goal, it would be a welcome opportunity and a great first step forward. Also, he could put it in his resumé.

TRISH

As college graduation approached, Trish worried that she did not have a range of employment opportunities to choose from like many of her classmates did. They all seemed busy with multiple career fairs and job interviews. All Trish had was a desire to support herself, without needing to brave the terrifying world of networking. She knew she would be bad at it. Talking to new people made her stomach hurt, and she never knew what to say. How could she manage networking events if she couldn't even

– Chapter 3 –

have a brief conversation with the librarian when she checked out a book? She thought about this problem long and hard during her hours in the tiny closet that was the intern office in her school's admissions department. Finally, she realized that she didn't need to network with everybody in the world, only with the one job she wanted, which was the one she had. She wrote an email to her internship supervisor, which was always much easier than talking face-to-face, and asked about the possibility of continuing to work there after graduation. It wasn't a huge leap into networking, but it was direct and focused on the job that was most important to her. If the answer was no, then she could expand her job-hunt networking, but she hoped she would never need to search beyond her college admissions department.

BILL

After graduation, Bill carefully constructed a portfolio with his resumé, letters of recommendation, and summaries of projects he'd completed in college. He purposefully kept it short, only the highlights, so that it fit easily into a flat folder. He made copies, fastened each one into a folder, and set off for a career expo at his university. As soon as he walked in the door, he felt overwhelmed and overstimulated. There were booths all around the walls of the large room, and tables in the center. He was visually distracted by colorful banners and easels with cardboard signs. Other job seekers were milling about, moving from booth to table, chatting with the recruiters. The sound of so many conversations going on simultaneously and bouncing off the high ceiling made it hard

Working While Autistic

to think. It was more than Bill could manage, so he left quickly, feeling like a failure. The next day, when he felt rested and stronger, he thought about the experience and what had been the worst part.

He hadn't known what to expect and was surprised by the sensory and social stimulation. It threw him off in a way that he couldn't easily recover from. At least now he knew what a large job fair was like. There was another one scheduled for the next week, so Bill prepared himself for it. He wore discreet loop-style earplugs to keep the noise level down, but he could still listen and talk to people. When he got there, he headed for the least-crowded corner of the room and found a table with no one else at it. The job recruiter would probably be relieved to have someone to talk to, so Bill felt confident enough to approach him and hand him a portfolio. Then the recruiter chatted with him and complimented him on the quality of his portfolio. Bill was pleased and felt able to engage in small talk for a short time before he moved on. He approached two other similarly un-busy tables, left them with copies of his portfolio, and then decided to leave; he had done as much as he could manage that day. Later he could attend another job fair with his plan to cope with the sensory and social stimulation and leave early. His approach to job fairs was different from that of all of the others crowding around the larger booths and tables, but it was right for him, and he counted it as a success.

– Chapter 3 –

MARIA

Maria knew what her perfect job would be: a proofreader, working from home. But where would she find someone to hire her? She didn't know anyone she could ask or network with, or where to even start. She decided to start where she usually did when she had a question: the internet. Her online job search showed her a lot of options for proofreading remotely from home. She sifted through them, passing by many large hiring companies that somehow seemed to stress her out with their hard-sell come-ons. Finally, she found a small, local self-publishing company whose authors often needed help with editing and proofreading. The publishers would send their proofreaders books to read as email attachments, and the proofreaders would correct grammar, punctuation, and word usage. This one felt just right to Maria. A small company was in her comfort zone.

ROBERT

Robert tried looking online for television repairman opportunities, but nowadays they called themselves technicians, not repairmen. He didn't see himself as a technician, and he hated those newfangled LCD thingies. He knew how to repair a good old cathode-ray tube (CRT) set, but you could hardly find them anymore. Still, he figured there must be some people left who held onto their old sets, and they'd need to be repaired if they broke. He had the skills, even if they were a bit old-fashioned. He needed to find a job where he could put his skills to work.

Working While Autistic

His online search turned up a lot of big store chains where you could buy a new TV, but when it broke, they just wanted to sell you a new one. Finally, he found a small, family-operated repair store. Maybe they could use him part-time. He was no good on the phone, so he decided to drive over there and see what the store was like.

Robert felt at home as soon as he walked in. It was cramped and dusty with shelves of used TVs and radios, floor to ceiling. He looked around, then approached the guy at the counter.

"Do you do television repairs on old CRT sets?" he asked.

"Well, we don't get much call for that these days. I mostly see the LCDs. If you need one fixed, it might take a while, because my guy who handles those is on a cross-country RV trip. He's mostly retired, but when he gets back, I can have him take a look at it for you."

"No, I do repairs myself. I'm retired from it, but I guess retirement isn't my cup of tea. I was hoping you needed some help. I wouldn't charge much, whatever you think is fair. You'd be doing my wife a favor if you'd get me out from under her feet." Both men chuckled.

"Well, sir, I'll give you a shot. Got an old set in the back. See what you can do with it."

Robert took the old set apart, tightened what needed tightening, and fixed what needed fixing. When he put it back together and turned it on, it worked like a charm, if you thought ancient TV sets were charming. Robert did.

The owner smiled, nodded, and reached out his hand. "I'm Guy, by the way."

– Chapter 3 –

Robert shook his hand. "Pleased to meet you, Guy. I'm Robert."

Guy wrote down his name and number and said he'd call if an old set came in for repair. This worked for Robert. Before he left, Guy said he was welcome to come hang out at the shop sometimes between jobs if he felt like it. Robert did, and left feeling on top of the world.

For Robert, having skills, finding a place that needed those skills, taking a chance on walking in cold without an appointment, and showing what he could do rather than talking about it got him back on the road to employment.

MESSAGES FROM AUTISTIC MENTORS

"I've searched for jobs frantically without a real plan when I needed money, but as I've gotten older, it's really important for me to take my time and make sure I will fit with the place. I will never go into customer service again."

— Helena, works with autistic children

"Don't just look for any job, because you will get burned out if it's not a good fit for you. If you love sneakers, don't try to work in a bookstore, and if you love books, don't try to sell sneakers. Look at your key interests, passion, or hyper-focus, and find companies that specialize in that."

— Suzanne, drive-through window greeter

Working While Autistic

"Have a CV or resumé tailored to the job you're applying for. If I'm looking for a writing job, I use a CV about writing, and if I'm looking for an animal care job, I use a CV tailored to animal care."
— Beth F. Watzke, late-diagnosed autistic writer and animal care provider

— CHAPTER 4 —
Interview
Be Yourself, But Not Like That!

"*"If you present as atypical ... consider being transparent about how you present ... Be self-confident in your self-awareness. It's a good thing to be self-aware."*

— *Samantha Craft*

One of the first steps down the road toward employment is the job interview. Most people feel anxious about interviews, so if you're nervous, you're not alone. It's one thing to write your skills and experience in a resumé or application, but to talk about them face-to-face is different. When you put your best foot forward, it can feel like you have to play a part, or mask. Everyone feels this way sometimes, including people in the neuro-majority. You want to let these strangers see that you would be a great addition to their team, so it makes sense to show them your best side. Perhaps you've been told, "Just be yourself," but then you realize that they only want you to be yourself when you don't make them uncomfortable. ("Not like that.") This is frustrating, and understandably so. It is not your job to make everyone else feel comfortable at the expense of your own comfort. However, a job interview is one time in your life when masking might be your best plan. We all want to make a good first impression in an interview.

There are things you can do to make a good first impression. Pay attention to the five Ps: *be prepared*, *be professional*, *be punctual*, *be positive*, and *provide a portfolio*.

THE 5 Ps TO BE

Prepared

The first P is to be *prepared*.

In his book, *Preparing for Life*, Dr. Jed Baker wrote, "It is crucial to develop a plan for having a successful interview." There are several important steps in the preparation process.

First, do your homework. Research the company. What is their primary purpose? What is their mission statement? Can you get behind it? If you already know what they're all about, it will give you an advantage.

Second, think about the questions they might ask you and how you'll answer. Most interviews include an open-ended invitation for you to talk about yourself. Stick to relevant, professional information, things that will help them realize you'd be a good fit for their job. Don't bring up your family, pets, hobbies, or anything else that is unrelated to the job you want. They'll probably ask about your strengths and weaknesses. Only share things that

Chapter 4

would affect your ability to do this job. If you're an expert in tae kwon do, it won't help you get a data-processing job. When you are prepared for questions they might ask, it shows them that you'd be a good team member.

Third, practice interviewing. If you can find a mock interview class, coach, or online interview prep service, consider it. Watch mock interviews on YouTube. Alternately, enlist friends and family to set up a mock interview experience for you. Remember to pretend that they're your real interviewers and behave as you would in the real thing. With practice comes familiarity. The more you practice, the more comfortable and less stressed you'll feel in your real interview.

Fourth, relax. I know, easier said than done, but there are things you can do to help you relax. Breathe mindfully to reduce anxiety. Before you get called in, when you're alone, exhale fully through your mouth so that it makes a slight "whoosh." Then close your mouth, inhale gently through your nose, and count to four. Hold your breath for a count of seven. On the eighth count, whoosh your breath out through your mouth again. Repeat the process, with your shoulders relaxed. If you're alone while you wait, consider striking a power pose, hands on your hips, feet apart and planted firmly, chin up, shoulders down. You should feel like a superhero doing this pose. You are strong, capable, and ready for anything!

Working While Autistic

Professional

The second P is to be *professional*.

You want to be seen as a serious professional who is the best person for the job. This means your physical presentation, including hygiene and clothing choices, should be impeccable. This is the time to dress like a boss. Avoid hats, shirts or jewelry with words, or extreme clothing. Select simplicity over flash. When you dress appropriately, you show that you're serious and professional.

You also want to be professional in your attitude. Greet your interviewers with your head up, look toward their eyes, and shake hands. The shake should be firm but not painful, accompanied by a single, unexaggerated, up-and-down movement. Don't shake hands too weakly with only your fingertips, or too powerfully, crushing their hands in your grip. Also, release promptly so that the handshake does not become a lengthy ordeal. If you are extremely uncomfortable shaking hands and cannot do this in an interview, be brief in your refusal. You might simply say, "I don't shake hands, but I am happy to meet you." Then move on without further explanation.

When seated, remain upright with your feet down or crossed neatly, close to your chair. Keep your back straight, shoulders down, head up, oriented toward your interviewers. Do not slouch, put your feet on any furniture, lean over sideways, stick your feet out in front of you, or hold your head down so they see the top of your head rather than your face. Look toward the person who asked the question first, and then let your glance move from person to

— Chapter 4 —

person while you answer. Don't focus only on the one across from you and ignore the others.

When you speak, modulate your volume, neither too loud nor too soft. Many autistic people don't realize that their normal voice is louder or quieter than average. Ask people who know you well if you need to fix the volume, and then practice so you can hit the right note.

Punctual

The third P is to be *punctual*.

The last thing you want to do is to arrive at your interview late so that your potential boss has to wait for you. They'll assume that if they hired you, you'd be late for work too. Plan how you will get to the interview. Will you drive, get a ride, take public transportation? Consider a practice run. How long does it take? How long would it take if there were extra traffic, or construction, or an accident? It's better to be early than late, so plan to be early enough that you won't be late even if all of these things happen. If you're way too early, wait in your car or find a nearby coffee shop where you can relax, read a book, and enjoy a cup of soothing herbal tea. Be sure to set an alarm or keep your watch visible so you don't miss your time.

Working While Autistic

Positive

The fourth P is to be *positive*.

This is the time to put your best foot forward. You'll be glad you prepared and practiced talking about your strengths, weaknesses, and how you handle mistakes.

When they ask for your strengths, honestly tell them the things you are good at that apply to this job. If you are an outstanding Dungeon Master (DM) for your Dungeons & Dragons (D&D) group, don't share that specifically, but do think about the skills that go in to being a good DM. Is it your ability to research and track information from various sources? Is it your attention to detail? Your respect for rules and standard operating procedures? Or is it your ability to focus on the task at hand? These strengths could be important in many careers, and that's what you want to talk about, not D&D.

When employers ask about your weaknesses, do not go overboard. This isn't a confessional, and you want them to hire you, so play this part down. They may ask you about a time you made a mistake, and how you handled it. Be prepared for this one. They want to know that you will be able to learn and grow from your mistakes. A good three-part response to errors is (1) admit your mistake; (2) fix your mistake; and (3) make a plan so that you don't repeat the mistake. They want to know that you can correct and learn from your mistakes. And don't disguise a brag as a fake weakness, like, "My weaknesses are that I work too hard and I give too much." This won't fool anyone, and it can put people off. Instead, have a realistic idea of your actual weaknesses, and

Chapter 4

be prepared to share briefly. If you are recently out of school, you could mention lack of experience as a weakness, but then let them know you are anxious to learn and gain experience. Don't claim to have no weaknesses (after all, you're human), but share what you have done to overcome a weakness. You might consider something like, "Because of my strong attention to detail, I have sometimes missed social cues, and I may come across as socially awkward. I've been working on this, and I welcome feedback as I continue to develop my skills." Any time you share a weakness that does not affect the position you are interviewing for and you describe how you have overcome it or turned it into a strength, it can work in your favor. Be careful not to share a weakness that would make you wrong for this job; for example, don't say you hate talking on the phone when applying for a telemarketing position.

It's at this point in the interview that some people choose to disclose their disability. The decision to disclose is a personal one, with pros and cons on both sides. We'll talk about this more in chapter 7. Whether or not you disclose that you're autistic, remember to stay positive and end on an uplifting note. Thank them for their time, smile, and shake hands again as you leave. Send a thank-you note or email later to thank them again for their time.

Portfolio

The fifth P is to provide a *portfolio*.

We brought this up in chapter 3, but it's important enough to mention again. Many autistic workers don't shine in interviews,

Working While Autistic

but their work product in the portfolio demonstrates their abilities. Let your work speak for you. Even if the job you want doesn't involve a physical product, a portfolio can still be a useful part of your interview process. If talking about yourself is not a great strength of yours, your portfolio can give interviewers something tangible.

Make sure your portfolio is neat and easy to navigate. A binder with plastic page protectors, rather than a file with random papers sticking out of it, can set a professional tone. So, what should you include in your job interview portfolio?

Start with an introduction cover page, including your name, contact information, and the position you want. This may change if you apply for a range of different kinds of jobs, and it's important to change your portfolio to reflect the current interview. Some people add a professional picture of themselves (not a vacation snapshot) to remind interviewers who you are when they make their decisions.

Next, include your updated resumé with relevant training and experience.

Be sure to have three references, people they can ask about you. If you've had a job before and you left on positive terms, list your previous bosses or supervisors. If you had a professor or teacher in school whose course is relevant to this job, you can list that person. Someone else that you've known a long time and can speak to your character, who is not related to you, could also be listed here. Do not list your parents, spouse, siblings, other close relatives, or friends you've never worked with. Be sure to ask each person

— Chapter 4 —

you list if they're willing to be a reference and ask what contact information they want you to share. Include any formal letters of recommendation here.

If the job you want is in a field such as graphic art, writing, design, or photography, include your best work samples. You want to let your work shine. If you worked on a special project and you have photographs that show your participation, include them with a brief description of the project. Be aware of others in the photographs, however, and do not share recognizable images of others without their permission. If you have photos of a school- or family-related project, make sure any children pictured have their back to the camera and are not identifiable. It's not okay to share other people's pictures without their permission. Finally, do not put in anything that is less than your best. This is where your work can make up for any awkwardness you may have felt in the face-to-face interview. On the last page of your portfolio, repeat your contact information and thank them for the opportunity. If possible, make copies and leave a portfolio for each of your interviewers to read later.

After the interview is over, plan for as much downtime as you can to decompress, de-stress, and recover from this intensely social and potentially stressful experience. You may have been masking hard, and now you can unmask. Do whatever helps you regulate, whether it's a video game, getting out in nature, or spending time alone in your room. Plan for that downtime. You've worked hard, and you deserve a break.

Working While Autistic

Let's see how our six characters managed the five Ps of the interview process.

SIX CHARACTERS IN SEARCH OF EMPLOYMENT

DAISY

DAISY: Mom! I'm home!

MOM: So you are. Did you get the classes you wanted this semester?

DAISY: Finally, there's a class that will be worth going to. I don't know why it took them until the last semester of senior year, but this is one class that might be useful.

MOM: That's encouraging. What is it?

DAISY: IRL Prep.

MOM: Explain?

DAISY: IRL is *in real life*. IRL Prep is "Survival Skills for Life After Graduation."

MOM: That does sound practical. What kind of things will you learn?

— Chapter 4 —

DAISY: Oh, you know, how to do things for yourself and become independent, instead of always expecting parents and teachers to do everything for us.

MOM: I like the sound of this.

DAISY: The final project is all about getting a job. We'll make portfolios and practice telling the class about them. We'll watch videos of mock interviews. The teacher is going to bring back some former students to tell us how they got their first jobs.

MOM: This sounds fascinating!

DAISY: But wait, there's more! We are going to do ... drumroll please ... mock interviews!

MOM: You sound excited about that. What do you think you'll like best about the mock interviews?

DAISY: Well, you know I get nervous talking to strangers.

MOM: I know.

DAISY: So this will give me a chance to practice, so that by the time I get to a real job interview, it'll be easy-peasy!

Working While Autistic

NARRATOR: *Daisy is right to be excited about such a course, applicable to real life the way no other classes before had ever been. Unlike algebra, this is one class she will really use.*

ZACH

Zach got the caretaker job! He liked working at the temple, but there wasn't much to do. Still, it was easy enough to unlock buildings and lock them back up at night, so he wasn't complaining. He knew someday he'd want something more, a real career, but he still wasn't sure what he wanted to do.

Noah, one of the other volunteers at their political party office, worked for an assisted living facility that provided services for disabled and elderly adults. Noah seemed to like it, and Zach wondered what it would be like to do that kind of work. When he asked, he learned that they had an opening for an assistant. It was part-time and didn't pay much, but he could keep his job at the temple. A letter of recommendation was required, so Zach decided to ask his rabbi for one.

As he sat in the rabbi's office, Zach thought back to his interview for the job he held now, in this very office. It wasn't a formal interview, more of a conversation about the job requirements, so Zach hadn't been particularly nervous. Interviewing with a stranger was different though. It made him anxious. He asked the rabbi why he had hired him in the first place. What had Zach said or done right that got him the job?

— Chapter 4 —

The rabbi told him it wasn't anything in particular, but that he'd known Zach since he was in Hebrew school and was glad to see him return to the temple as a young adult. He always saw potential in Zach, but he also knew that it wouldn't be easy for a shy, awkward young man to get a job. The rabbi wanted to give him a boost. Now, he wrote Zach a glowing recommendation, which addressed his character and integrity as well as his capability. Zach thanked him and admitted he was afraid he would mess up the interview.

"Zach, Zach, Zach." The rabbi put his hand on his shoulder. "*Al tira*. Have no fear. Remember that the person across the desk is another child of God, as you are. Christians, Muslims, Jews, we all worship the same God. Remember that you are formed from the same dust and you need not fear. But remember this as well, for this also is important," he added.

"What is it, Rabbi?"

"Get a better haircut."

Zach smiled. "I will," he said, "and thank you."

Zach did get a haircut before his job interview for the assisted living facility position. When he realized there would be two people on the interview panel instead of one, it threw him off a bit, but he recovered. He remembered the rabbi's encouraging words, took a couple of slow breaths, and sat down to answer their questions. It went much better than he had feared, and he was filled with relief as he walked out. The next day, he wrote them a simple thank-you letter and prepared himself to wait for their decision.

Working While Autistic

TRISH

Soon after she emailed her internship supervisor about applying for a full-time position in the admissions department after graduation, she received an application form to fill out. Her hands trembled as she held it, and then she filled it out in her best block printing and turned it in quickly, before she could lose her courage. Within two days, she already had an interview appointment. Trish was both terrified and exhilarated. This was what she wanted, and she didn't want to let her fear get in the way.

She sought out her internship supervisor for advice and shared her nervousness. Her supervisor advised her to be prepared to answer questions about her strengths and weaknesses, but not to dwell too long on her weaknesses. She knew Trish was likely to confess all of her shortcomings without mentioning any of the things she could do well. She asked Trish to tell her about the strengths she brought to the job during her internship, and supplemented with what she had observed when Trish couldn't think of any strengths. For instance, she was punctual, loyal, always did her best, and completed every project within the deadline. As far as weaknesses are concerned, her supervisor recommended that she think of only one that might affect the job and follow it with what she was doing to improve in that area. Trish decided to share as a weakness that she was shy with people and preferred to work alone, but that she was aware of this and working on it.

After her session with her supervisor, Trish felt much more confident in her ability to survive the interview process. She would plan plenty of time beforehand to prepare and relax, as well as a

— Chapter 4 —

lengthy recovery time afterward, with no classes, studying, or other engagements for at least a day or two after the interview. With the right preparation, Trish felt she could do this.

BILL

Bill was relieved that one of the few people he had spoken to at the job fair wanted to interview him. He'd researched the company, and it seemed like a good fit for him. He was anxious to make a good first impression at the interview. He packed a few more copies of his portfolio into a messenger bag, put on a jacket and tie, and headed off to the interview. He'd already made a couple of practice runs to the office building during the week before the interview, so he knew exactly how long it would take him to get there and where the office was. He arrived, still twenty minutes early, greeted the receptionist, and sat down to wait.

The door opened with a bang, and a young man with moussed hair, a three-piece suit, and a slim attaché case strode in. He looked down at the receptionist and said, "Well, I'm here, and I don't have all day." He seemed to expect her to know who he was and looked irritated when he had to tell her his name. He became belligerent when she told him that, since he was twenty minutes late for his appointment time, they would not interview him today after all. After he insulted her intelligence, he swore and stormed out. Bill felt terrible for the receptionist, but she maintained her composure. When it was his turn and she showed him to the interview room, he thanked her, calling her by her name, which was on her desk.

Working While Autistic

Bill felt like he didn't do too badly during the interview, but he was still nervous. As he left, the receptionist waved him over.

"Don't look so worried," she told him. "I have a feeling you've got a good chance here."

"I don't know," he said. "That other guy looked really important."

"Maybe he thought so, but around here, how people treat each other goes a long way. I'm sure the entire interview panel heard his performance out here. You won't have much competition from him, I guarantee it."

Bill thanked her, feeling a bit more confident. He hoped she was right.

MARIA

Maria was excited about a career as an at-home proofreader. The only problem was going to the office for the interview. It made her nervous, but she'd have to go through with it if she wanted the job.

On the day of her interview, Maria dressed carefully. Her dress was dark blue, with a high neck and a hemline that reached below her knees, and she wore simple black flats. She wanted to appear professional, and she didn't want anything she wore to call attention to itself or be distracting. She hoped for, and achieved, anonymity of presentation.

She arrived a bit early for her appointment time and waited in the foyer to be called into the office. It was a relief to be early rather than late. Maria hated to be late for anything.

When she was called in, she saw the interviewers were dressed more casually than she was. The men wore slacks and polo shirts,

– Chapter 4 –

and the women wore tasteful trousers with brightly colored blouses and chunky jewelry. They made Maria feel at home and welcome. She'd taken the proofreading test they sent her, and they were impressed with her skills. They hired her on the spot and told her she could work from home except for the required monthly staff meetings.

Maria was elated! It seemed like the perfect job for her. By being punctual, demonstrating her skills, and paying attention to her personal presentation, Maria showed herself to be professional and the best person for the job.

ROBERT

After about a week of hanging out at the TV repair shop, the owner told Robert that his CRT guy wasn't coming back. He and his wife liked the RV life so much they were making it permanent. That left a part-time opening.

Robert was definitely interested. They scheduled an interview, and he even put on a tie for it. He felt silly, since they usually wore T-shirts and baseball caps around the store, but an interview was different, somehow. More formal.

The owner managed not to laugh when he saw Robert in a tie, but he said it showed gumption; he must really want the job if he was willing to wear that choker. The interview itself didn't take long. He'd already seen what Robert could do, so the owner didn't have many questions. He hired him based on his on-the-job performance. That was a huge relief to Robert, because he knew he wasn't so great with small talk. By demonstrating what he could

Working While Autistic

do on the job and showing he was serious by dressing up for the interview, he was hired.

MESSAGES FROM AUTISTIC MENTORS

"I'm sure other people do interviews better than I do, but I usually try to prepare a few things that are specific to the job I'm applying for, so I don't just ramble. After the interview, I spend the whole next day recovering and doing soothing activities to de-stimulate myself."

— Helena, works with autistic children

"Interviewing is one of my weak spots. I'd rather make a PowerPoint presentation that will answer the questions that they usually ask in interviews and highlight my skills, rather than having to answer questions as they are asked in an interview. This idea, helping people create interview presentations, is a future dream of mine."

— Suzanne, drive-through window greeter

"If I think of the job interview as an audition and draw on my theater background, it helps me. It's a positive use of masking. I wish I didn't have to mask at all, but if I think of it that way, it's more positive and fun, and I don't get so nervous."

— Beth F. Watzke, late-diagnosed autistic writer and animal care provider

– PART II –
On the Job

"No, autism is not a 'gift.' For most, it is an endless fight against schools, workplaces, and bullies. But, under the right circumstances, given the right adjustments, it *can* be a superpower."
— *Greta Thunberg* —

"The expert in anything was once a beginner."
— *Helen Hayes* —

— CHAPTER 5 —
You're Hired!
Now What?

"Work offers an excellent opportunity for autistic people to develop their social and life skills, but it's important, too, to find the right job that will help you thrive."

— *Ambitious About Autism*

You've got the job. Congratulations! Now what?

Well, the obvious answer is, do the job. This means putting into daily practice everything you've learned along the road. Here's how to succeed in business:

Remember the five Ps of interviewing? If you want to succeed in whatever career you choose, you'll still need four of them: *be punctual*, *be professional*, *be prepared*, and *be positive*. Each of these four Ps is slightly different at work, as compared to the interview process.

Working While Autistic

BE PUNCTUAL

Punctuality is important in any career. You're paid to be on the job on time. If it's hard for you to get out of bed in the morning, there are things you can do. Don't continue to rely on a parent to get you out the door. Now that you're an adult, that responsibility is yours. Here are four tips to prioritize punctuality:

Punctuality Tip #1: Set multiple alarms.

If you're one of those people who find alarms jarring, find one that's pleasant but will still wake you up. You may need to invest in another device or an app if there are no sound options on your phone that work for you. Some people prefer to have a soft light come on gradually in the room, or a gentle vibration. Some place their alarm clock across the room so they can't turn it off in their sleep. If you know you need extra time to adjust to the morning, then plan that into your schedule. Set your first alarm early enough that you can hit snooze and still get out the door on time.

Punctuality Tip #2: Get plenty of sleep the night before.

This can be tricky if you struggle with insomnia, as many autistic folk do. Most adults need seven to nine hours of sleep a night, but your needs may be slightly different. Document how you feel after a night with only five or six hours of sleep, as compared to ten to eleven hours. Once you know how much sleep is best for you, count backward from the time you need to get up to see what

— Chapter 5 —

time you should go to sleep the night before. If you take an hour to wind down before you actually fall asleep, add that hour in. Once you know what time you need to go to bed, remind yourself to do it. This is another time when a phone alarm or app can help you. Research sleep hygiene and put into practice the tips that are most helpful for you.

Punctuality Tip #3: Make a rule for yourself.

If you are the kind of person who thrives on a code of rules, make one that serves you. The rule might be to only hit snooze twice. After the second snooze, you must get out of bed, because that's the rule.

Punctuality Tip #4: Reward yourself.

If a fancy coffee on your way to work is in your budget and supports your health, then plan to reward yourself with a cup of your favorite brew. Only do this when you have allowed plenty of time to pick it up on your way. When you run late, make do with the coffee in the staff room at work and plan to get up earlier the next day. Coffee is not the best reward for everyone, so personalize it. Use whatever makes you happy as your reward. Keep track of every day that you arrive on time, and at the end of the week or month, if you arrive on time every workday, celebrate your success. Don't expect your boss to notice when you're on time, or to be praised for it; that's a normal part of your job. On the other hand, if you arrive late, it will be noticed. Be ready to do what it takes to arrive on time every day.

Working While Autistic

BE PROFESSIONAL

For your interview, you probably dressed up. Once you have the job, the dress code may (or may not) be more relaxed. Notice how other people at your level of employment dress. Present yourself professionally at a level commensurate with or slightly above your position. You can find clothing that looks professional but feels comfortable. Find what's best for you.

You may prefer to wear the same outfit every day. Don't do it. Even if you could buy five identical shirts or dresses and wear a different, clean one every day, people will think you're wearing the same, unwashed outfit. If you've found a comfortable piece of clothing, buy it in five different colors, not five identical pieces.

If your office has an established casual Friday, make sure you know what that means. You don't want to show up on your first Friday in yoga pants, a T-shirt, and flip-flops only to find that everyone else is in dress slacks and a jacket but no tie. Also, not every company even has casual Friday. If you work with customers or attend meetings with higher-ups all week, you probably won't have casual Friday. Don't assume Friday will be different from other days.

BE PREPARED

If you've been given a work assignment and it's time to present your results to your boss, make sure you've done your homework and

— Chapter 5 —

prepared everything in advance. Being prepared means knowing what's expected, and having the deadlines on your calendar. Prepare properly, and you won't be caught off guard.

BE POSITIVE

The optimistic employee whose glass is half full is appreciated. The negative one who's overly critical may find that people avoid them. They may even be passed over for promotions.

If you are anxious by nature, try to channel your anxiety into positivity. When you start to feel fearful, think about what that feels like for you. Is your heart pounding, are you breathing rapidly? Can you feel increased blood flow or an adrenaline rush? This means your body wants to take care of you. If your body thinks you're in danger, it will rally to prepare you for battle. Tell yourself, "My body wants to support me. It's ready for anything, even though there's no real danger. Thanks, body, but we're okay."

Reframe your emotions with different words to describe how you feel. Instead of, "I'm nervous," tell yourself, "I'm excited." The physical response of excitement is almost identical to that of anxiety. Your attitude may imperceptibly change as you use more positive words or phrases to label what's going on inside of you.

When you have an opportunity to speak up and say something, use the triple filter test, which has been attributed to Socrates, the poet Rumi, and others. Ask yourself three questions: Is it true? Is it good? Is it useful? If your answer is yes to all three of these questions,

Working While Autistic

then go ahead and speak up. When someone says whatever pops into their heads with no filter, it can come across as rude. When you choose your words carefully, you can put a positive spin on what you share at work. You can always go home and pour your heart out to your dog or significant other, but don't vent at work. Keep it positive and upbeat.

When you're punctual, professional, prepared, and positive, you're on the road to success in your new job. Let's see how our six fictional characters did.

SIX CHARACTERS IN SEARCH OF EMPLOYMENT

DAISY

NARRATOR: *It is an honor to be chosen as a part-time after-school employee of Lilacs & Lattes, the florist/nursery/coffee shop. Daisy proudly dons her new apron, moss green with cursive L & L stitched out in purple thread. This is her new armor! She enters the establishment, eager to start her first day on the job.*

LILAC: You're late.
(owner)

DAISY: No, I'm—I mean, I don't think so. You told me to start at 3:30, and I left school at 3:30 on the

– Chapter 5 –

DAISY: dot. It took me 10 minutes to walk here, so here I am, 3:40 exactly.
(continued)

LILAC: When I said you start at 3:30, I meant you start working at 3:30, not start walking to work.

NARRATOR: *It is with horror that our hero realizes her error. In hindsight, it seems obvious, but at the time, she thought "start at 3:30" meant "start walking to work at 3:30." Was this how she was to start her first day of gainful employment? Would she be fired before she began? What did fate have in store for the hapless Daisy?*

DAISY: Oh no, I am so sorry! That was stupid of me. I should have realized. Don't worry, that will never happen again! I'll be early every day from now on!

LILAC: Don't worry, you're here now. I'm glad to see you've already got your apron on. Put away your bag in the back, and you can start stocking the seed packets that just came in. I'll show you where they go.

NARRATOR: *Daisy feels intense relief at not being fired, and mortification at her egregious error. The two battling emotions are overwhelming. She really wants to keep this job. It's a quiet shop, never*

Working While Autistic

NARRATOR: *crowded, but never boring. Perfect for her. After*
(continued) *she puts away her bag, she closes her eyes and takes several slow, deep breaths before coming back out to start work. She is going to be okay. In fact, she's going to be better than okay. The smell of espresso, the colors of the floral bouquets, the way the light filters through the leaves of the forest of potted plants, Daisy is in heaven.*

Over time, Daisy would move from stocking, to repotting plants, to working with customers and creating bouquets and floral displays. Eventually, she'd even learn to be a barista, frothing and frapping with ease. Lilac taught her everything with patience, and Daisy could tell that she trusted her.

NARRATOR: *Mayhap one day our hero will have her own florist/nursery/coffee shop. What will she call it? Daisies and Dregs? No, that sounds terrible. Daisies and Decaf? Nope. Daisies and Dark Roast? It doesn't have to be Daisies, does it? She won't copy Lilac's idea. How about Fresh Grounds? Coffee Potters? Brewing and Blooming? Greens and Beans? Fronds and Froths? No need to decide today; Daisy has her future ahead of her with plenty of time. For now, she loves her after-school job and all the real-life experience points she is earning.*

– Chapter 5 –

ZACH

During his first week at the assisted living facility, Zach noticed that every time he started talking at length about his favorite topics, such as his frustration with politics and the world situation, the break room would get quiet. He was giving in to the temptation to vent, but maybe not everyone there shared his feelings. Also, it started to sound like he was complaining all the time. That wasn't professional, and it wasn't the impression he wanted to give. He'd better change this habit so he wouldn't put people off with a lot of negative venting.

The next day, he wore three large rubber bands around his wrist. They weren't tight enough to hurt, but he was aware of them, and he wrote a letter on each band: T for *true*, K for *kind*, and N for *necessary*. He wanted to remind himself to ask three questions before he said anything. Is it true? Is it kind or good? Is it necessary or useful? If the answer to even one of those was no, he would keep it to himself. If he needed to vent, he could wait until he got home and talk about it on one of his online chat rooms where everyone shared his feelings.

Zach wanted to be careful not to let his tendency to talk about negative things affect his work environment. It didn't feel professional; he wanted to be upbeat so they wouldn't think he was a downer. The rubber band wrist reminders kept him on track with his new positive attitude.

Meanwhile, he still had his job at the temple to pay attention to. Zach listened to the voicemail message from the temple trustee and then replayed it a few times to make sure he understood. The

Working While Autistic

trustee said that the fire department would contact him for the annual fire extinguisher inspection and that Zach should arrange a time with them. On the day of the inspection, Zach was to go with the inspector through all of the buildings, unlock each room, and wait while they inspected the fire extinguishers and attached certification tags. When they were all done, Zach should make sure all the rooms were locked again and notify the trustee that it had been completed.

No problem. Zach arranged the inspection for the next day at a time that wouldn't interfere with his second job. He followed the inspector to each room and saw that each fire extinguisher had been tagged and the rooms locked up. Then Zach went to the offices. The rabbi's door was open, and he was reading scripture.

"Everything's all taken care of," Zach said from the doorway.

"Pardon?" The rabbi looked up and adjusted his glasses.

"All of the fire extinguishers have been inspected. All taken care of," Zach repeated.

"Well, that's nice. Thank you." The rabbi returned to his reading.

Two weeks later, he was called into the office by the trustee. He looked stern and said, "Zach, I'm sorry, but this arrangement doesn't seem to be working out. We need a caretaker who can be responsible for taking on assignments in a timely manner. When you ignored my call about the fire extinguisher inspection, you put us at legal risk for noncompliance."

"What do you mean? I didn't ignore it; I took care of it the next day." Zach was confused and concerned. It sounded like they were going to fire him.

— Chapter 5 —

"I left you a message on your phone, and you never replied. I asked you to tell me when it was taken care of, and I have heard nothing."

"The day after you left the message, they did all of the inspections and put on all of the tags. Then I came straight over to the office and told the rabbi it was taken care of."

"You told the rabbi? Why would you tell the rabbi about fire extinguishers?"

"Well, I came over to the office, and I didn't see you, but the rabbi was here. So I told him."

"You told the rabbi instead of telling me, as I had asked?" He seemed incredulous.

Zach looked down, embarrassed. It had made sense to him at the time, but now it seemed foolish. "I guess I thought he would tell you, since you all work together. I made a mistake. I should have told you, not the rabbi."

"That is correct. A rabbi is not a message boy. From now on, if I leave you a message, please reply immediately that you have received it and that you will act on it. And if I ask you to get back to me, do not go through the rabbi. He has enough to do."

Zach was relieved he hadn't been fired. He thanked the trustee and promised to do better. He didn't like talking on the phone, but he could do it now that he knew how important it was. Being the temple caretaker wasn't his long-term career goal, but he'd better improve his communication skills if he wanted to move up in the world. And he knew he could.

Working While Autistic

TRISH

Trish got the Admissions job! Apparently, she was the only one surprised by this. On her first day entering the campus as a regular, full-time employee, not a student intern, she was determined to rise to her new position. She decided to dress more professionally, less like a college student, matching the other women she worked with. She was also determined to show that she could be a team player, sort of. At least she could acknowledge her coworkers when she saw them in the office, rather than shrinking into corners, acting like a scared mouse. Every day now, she walked into the building with her head high and greeted everyone she saw. She had been worried about how to greet people appropriately, which is why she usually avoided it altogether.

Finally, she decided that a simple, "Good morning," directed toward each person with a smile would be sufficient. Upon leaving, she could simply say, "Good night, see you tomorrow," or on Fridays, "Have a good weekend, see you on Monday." Having a plan for how to greet people gave her confidence each time she entered the building. She was a real professional now, not an intern, and she belonged.

BILL

Bill hated answering the phone, but when he saw the call was from the manager where he'd interviewed the week before, he picked up the call rather than letting it go to voicemail. He hoped he didn't sound too shaky, and he kept his replies short to keep himself from nervously over-talking.

— Chapter 5 —

It was good news! He was hired for the computer tech position he'd applied for. He would start Monday, just six days away. Bill tried to get plenty of rest during those six days and not stress too much about the new job. He showed up early on his first day, and the receptionist he had spoken with before waved him over.

"Congratulations! Mr. Brisbee will be here in about ten minutes to show you your station and introduce you around."

"Thank you," Bill was grateful she remembered him. He'd had a nightmare about walking in on the first day and being ignored by everyone as if he were invisible. It was nice to be remembered and expected.

In spite of his usual level of discomfort when in groups of people, Bill enjoyed being introduced to the other computer techs, and he was pleased there was a workstation ready for him. There was a lot of information to read that first day, including the employee handbook and standard operating procedures (SOPs). There was nothing Bill appreciated more than SOPs. You knew what to expect and what was expected of you. Learning about the way his department worked, who he reported to, how he would get his assignments, and what to do after a task was completed gave him confidence. Being prepared confirmed for Bill that this was a job he could do.

MARIA

Maria loved her new job, but she dreaded going to her first staff meeting. What should she wear? How should she act? Should she say anything, or be quiet the whole time? She wanted to be

Working While Autistic

professional and fit in. Attending meetings was something new for her, and that increased her anxiety. At least it would be in the same room where she had interviewed for the job, so the place would be familiar, and some of the people, too. She reminded herself of what would be familiar each time she started to feel nervous. She also brought a small key chain of a sloth and one of a robot. They would stay hidden in her purse, but knowing they were there reminded her to be calm like a sloth and fearless like a giant robot.

On the day of the staff meeting, Maria took a long time choosing what to wear. She remembered how comfortable and casual the interviewers had been, and she felt that her wardrobe was stuffy and buttoned-up in comparison. She didn't own any clothes that were casual, except the kinds of things she would wear around the house or to pick up the newspaper and mail. Those things were far too informal and shabby. She finally chose a dark rose-colored dress and added a floral scarf her daughters had given her for her birthday. It seemed cheerful and in line with what she'd seen the others wear, but true to the simple style she was comfortable with.

When she got to the meeting, she found an empty chair as far as possible from the head of the table. She accepted an offer to help herself to the coffee and refreshments, because stirring coffee and holding a cup gave her something to do with her hands. She smiled vaguely and nodded to the others as they came in, but she didn't initiate conversation. It was hard enough to be in this place without trying to manage small talk too. Once the meeting started, she relaxed a bit. She was surprised when the boss introduced her as their newest team member, and she gave a little wave, blushing

— Chapter 5 —

when they looked at her and clapped. They seemed glad to have her join their company.

Maria glanced at the other women in the room periodically to see what they were doing so she could imitate them. They sat oriented toward the person speaking and occasionally nodded at a point they agreed on or laughed at a joke. Maria was surprised at how often one or another of them spoke up and offered ideas or suggestions. They seemed so confident. Maria would not be doing that herself, preferring the sidelines, but she found it gratifying to work in a company that valued the women's ideas as much as the men's.

After the meeting was over, Maria was relieved to go back to working from home until the next month. She had effectively used her people skills to observe and imitate what others did in the meeting. She also tried to match her choice of outfit to what she had seen other women wearing, but without sacrificing her personal style and comfort. These skills helped her fit in rather than stand out, which was right for her. She felt like a real professional.

ROBERT

It felt great being back in the workforce, even if it was part-time. Retirement didn't sit well with Robert; he craved the familiarity of going to work and the satisfaction of doing a job well. His workplace was so casual he never felt uncomfortable, and his boss was easy-going and seemed to like him. If he noticed any social awkwardness or quirks, he never mentioned them. It was the ideal workplace for an old geezer like Robert.

Working While Autistic

What worked best for Robert was to be prepared for whatever task his boss tossed his way. He brought his own tools; he'd worked with them for so long that they fit his hand like an extension of his arm. Having the tools he needed helped him feel ready to take on anything.

MESSAGES FROM AUTISTIC MENTORS

"I've had a lot of different jobs over the years, and I learned that customer service is not for me. Working with autistic students, I can relate to them and make a difference."

— Helena, works with autistic children

"My very first job in 1986 was at a McDonald's. It was nothing but cleaning tables and washing floors, with no intellectual stimulation. I've worked in retail too. Working at the drive-through window is the right fit for me."

— Suzanne, drive-through window greeter

"My first job was at a county fair in the Midwest. I was a waitress, and I liked it because it was outdoors and I enjoyed the one-on-one interactions with the customers. The smells, the people, and especially all the animals made it a very positive environment."

— Beth F. Watzke, late-diagnosed autistic writer and animal care provider

– CHAPTER 6 –
Work Ethic
Learn to HERD CATS

"Our success should depend not on accident of birth, but the strength of our work ethic and the scope of our dreams."

— *Barack Obama*

Now that you have your first job, you'll want to make sure you keep it, at least as long as you want to. One way to ensure that your employer wants to keep you around is to have a good work ethic. Work ethic is one of those things that is difficult to describe but important to have if you want to be successful in your career. It includes being motivated from within to do a good job even when no one is watching. People with good work ethic don't rely on external rewards or praise to do their job, although most of us appreciate it. They take personal pride in doing their work and doing it well. Some people say that if you don't already have it, developing work ethic is as difficult as trying to herd cats.

Working While Autistic

But you can do difficult things, can't you?

Remember HERD CATS for the qualities you need to nurture in yourself to improve your work ethic. HERD CATS stands for *honesty, excellence, responsibility, discipline, communication, accepting authority, teamwork*, and *solution-focused*.

HERD CATS

Honesty

The H in HERD CATS is for *honesty*.

There are two sides to honesty in the workplace.

First, it's important to tell the truth if you messed up. Don't lie to protect yourself or try to shift the blame to someone else. Honesty shows maturity, and it's important if you want to advance in your chosen career.

On the other hand, you must be wise about when you use the two-edged sword of honesty. If you say things to your colleagues that are true but unkind, such as telling someone that their gross tuna sandwich stinks up the whole office and you want to vomit every time you walk by their desk, feelings will be hurt. Your coworkers may even turn against you and gossip about you behind your back.

Another pitfall of honesty is if you tell your supervisor that they have made a mistake in a way that embarrasses them. If they misspoke about some small detail that will not affect the company in the long run, keep it to yourself. If you interrupt to say the

— Chapter 6 —

last meeting wasn't on a Tuesday, it was on a Thursday, it may be accurate, but it will work against you. On the other hand, if you see your boss is about to make a mistake that could have serious and costly consequences for the business, you must tell them, but do so privately. Don't call them out in front of other workers, and don't go over their head to the big boss. Either of these will cause negative reactions. People have lost their jobs over this kind of thing. Before you bring out your honesty sword, ask yourself if it is kind or unkind, and if it is necessary or merely a detail that won't make a difference in the long run.

Excellence

The E in HERD CATS is for *excellence*.

No matter what you do, it's vital to do your job with a goal of excellence. There's a story about the first time President Kennedy visited NASA in 1962. They say he saw a custodian with a broom and asked him what he did at NASA. The custodian's reply? "I'm helping to put a man on the moon." Now, I don't know if this story happened in exactly this way, or if it ever happened at all, but like so many stories that are told and retold over the years, it has a message that resonates with people. The custodian in the story saw his job as more than just sweeping the floors and emptying the trash. He recognized that what he did was vital for the smooth operation of NASA so that the scientists could do their job. The result was that we did put a man on the moon, and everyone involved helped make it happen, from the rocket scientists to the custodial staff. Because he held that attitude about his job, he probably completed

Working While Autistic

each task with care and excellence, never sloppy or neglectful of his duties. Whatever your work, whether you've just started off on the bottom rung of your career ladder, partway up, or at the top ready to retire, doing your work with excellence is important. It's not only for your boss, your customers, or the company, but it's also for your own self-respect. You and your work are important. Let your excellent light shine!

Responsibility

The R in HERD CATS is for *responsibility*.

Responsibility is an adult attribute. Children are not particularly responsible. Their parents tell them when to wake up, eat, do chores, and go to bed. Their teachers tell them what to do at school. If they make a mistake, they might lie or blame someone else to escape punishment. This is childish, which is understandable in the very young, but more responsibility is expected of adults.

Adults must be responsible for arriving at work on time and remaining productive throughout their hours of employment, doing the job they were hired to do. When they take their break, they return to work after break time is up. When they need to take a sick day, they notify their supervisor as soon as possible. They know if they fail to show up for their shift without notice, it causes problems for everyone. Sometimes neurodivergent employees experience a lot of stress in their jobs, and it can be debilitating. Some have tried hiding because they need time to self-regulate. It's okay to go to the restroom during your break and stim or sit in your car during lunch with your eyes closed. It's not okay for a

– Chapter 6 –

warehouse worker to climb on top of the high shelves and take a nap where they can't be seen. It's not okay to go out for your thirty-minute lunch break and stay away for a couple of hours. People have been fired for this. If the stress of your job is getting to you, be responsible. Talk to your employer about needed accommodations, rather than avoiding work. You deserve to have a safe, supportive, and accommodating work environment.

Another aspect of responsibility is to own up to your own mistakes. If you are reprimanded, don't blame someone else or accuse your supervisor of not explaining the task well enough. The responsible thing is to say that you'll do better next time, and then follow up so you don't repeat the same mistakes. Two important aspects of an effective apology are first, admit your mistake, and second, make a plan to ensure it doesn't happen again.

Discipline

The D in HERD CATS is for *discipline*.

H. Jackson Brown Jr. wrote, "Talent without discipline is like an octopus on roller skates. There's plenty of movement, but you never know if it's going to be forward, backwards, or sideways." Chances are you have a lot of talent already. But do you have control of that roller skating octopus to make your talent work for you instead of rolling you down one rabbit hole after another? It takes discipline to stick with something that is hard or boring. But if you're paid to do a job, discipline is an important feature of work ethic. Self-management strategies come in handy here. (If you want to learn more, there's a chapter about self-management in

Working While Autistic

Independent *Living While Autistic*, the first book in this *Adulting While Autistic* series.)

Communication
The C in HERD CATS stands for *communication*.

Communication is essential to any work experience. A major feature of autism is that communicating with the neuro-majority can be challenging. Communicating with other autistic folk is usually not a problem. So how can you communicate with your neuro-majority coworkers and supervisors without misunderstanding them or being misunderstood? Seek clarity and stick to business.

When you communicate with coworkers, try to limit communication to work-related topics most of the time. Avoid involvement with office gossip, politics, or anything negative. It's smart to stay out of it when there's drama in the break room.

That said, it can be good practice to ask and answer simple questions such as, "How was your weekend?" on a Monday, and, "Do you have any weekend plans?" on a Friday. If someone asks you one of these questions, you're not obligated to share anything personal that you'd rather keep to yourself. Consider having a stock answer at the ready, such as, "I'm looking forward to a quiet weekend," or, "I had a good weekend, thanks." Then be sure to ask them the same question back. If someone had a special weekend or has exciting plans for the weekend to come, they usually can't wait to share it. After they ask you about your weekend, they look forward to sharing their own news. If you answer without

Chapter 6

returning the same question back to them, they may feel like you left them hanging.

When you communicate with supervisors, managers, or bosses, ask for clarity when given instructions that seem ambiguous or unclear to you. Then follow it up with an email. Write a brief message such as, "I'm writing to clarify our conversation this morning. I understand you need me to do (*task*) and turn it in to (*person*) by (*date*). Is this correct? Thank you." Then they have a chance to set you right if what you wrote was not what they meant, and you both have a written, dated record of the assignment in the email. Be sure to reply to their clarification to let them know you are on it and will have it finished by the deadline. Save all of your task-clarification emails in a folder so you can refer to them when needed, and to make sure you don't forget any of them.

Accept Authority

The A in HERD CATS stands for *accept authority*.

Accepting authority is another important part of work ethic. When you're given a task that you don't see any reason for, it feels natural to resist it until your manager explains why it's important to do. However, if you ask them right off the bat why you should do it, they might think you're defiant or disrespectful. Most managers don't take kindly to being questioned about assignments they give; it feels like insubordination to them, and employees have lost their jobs over this. Even if a task doesn't make sense to you, when a person in authority tells you to do something, lead with, "Yes, I can do that. When do you need it completed?" This will show them that you have a good work ethic. Later, if you really can't see any reason for the task, you may email politely for clarification of the purpose, to help you to do your best job. If no clarification is given, go ahead and do the task anyway, whether or not you agree with it. The exception here would be if the task is illegal or unethical or goes against your moral principles. Think carefully, though, before you take a stand on moral grounds for an otherwise legal task. Look at it from your employer's point of view. For example, if a worker says that they cannot serve a particular customer because of their religious beliefs, then it would be in the company's best interest to hire someone else who could serve all customers of every faith. Accepting authority will make you a more valued employee, and it shows good work ethic.

Teamwork

The T in HERD CATS stands for *teamwork*.

One of the most challenging aspects of working while autistic is the expectation for teamwork. One way to look at teamwork is the idea that you all work for the same company (team) and you share common goals. This attitude of shared vision for the overall success of the company is important.

Another kind of teamwork might include being assigned to group tasks. In school, you might have hated group assignments. Maybe you ended up doing all the work yourself, or maybe the other team members ignored your input. Either way, group assignments might be something you were glad to leave behind when you graduated. Now that you're in the workforce, if you get assigned

— Chapter 6 —

to a team, it might come as a disappointment. Don't immediately reject the assignment, though, or you might be seen as problematic. Give it a try. If you tried but group tasks don't work for you, talk to your supervisor. If your employer knows that you are autistic and therefore eligible for accommodations under the Americans with Disabilities Act (ADA), you might ask for individual tasks rather than group tasks. If they don't know about your autism and you choose not to disclose this, you could tell them that you're the kind of person who does your best work independently and you are most productive on your own. They may or may not accommodate you.

When you are given a task and you say you'll do it right away and then have it finished by the deadline, that demonstrates your commitment to the greater team of the company you work for.

Solution Focused

The S in HERD CATS stands for being *solution focused*.

When there's a problem in the workplace, if it can't be easily solved on your own, you have the right to seek support. When you do so, though, it's smart to come from a position of offering possible solutions. Someone who always complains but doesn't have any ideas to solve the problem becomes annoying pretty quickly. Being focused on solutions rather than problems shows good work ethic.

Working While Autistic

SIX CHARACTERS IN SEARCH OF EMPLOYMENT

DAISY

NARRATOR: *Our hero enters the portal of the world of the future: Workability class, fifth period. Her steps are sluggish as she tries to hide among the horde of students. For on this day, for the first time in this class, Daisy has forgotten her homework. She slips into her seat and avoids eye contact with the teacher while other students place their completed homework into the finished work basket.*

MR. WORTH: Daisy, where's your homework?

DAISY: *(Looks up like a guilty squirrel caught in the headlights.)* Um, what?

MR. WORTH: I was just asking where your homework is.

DAISY: Oh, sure. It's, um, I guess it's in the finished work basket. That's where it's supposed to be, right?

MR. WORTH: Would you take it out and give it to me, please?

DAISY: *(Freezes, stares blankly, finally finds her voice.)* You mean, give it to you now? Can't you just look at it with all the others, after school?

— Chapter 6 —

MR. WORTH: Please come up and find it in the basket for me. I didn't see you put it in, but you said you did, so I'd like you to find it for me.

DAISY: Well, it must be in there somewhere. It's due today, right?

MR. WORTH: Right. Please hand it to me.

NARRATOR: *Our hero shuffles forward as slowly as a Shrieking Toad with a move speed of zero. She thumbs through the homework papers in the basket.*

DAISY: Hm. I don't see it here.

MR. WORTH: I'm not surprised.

DAISY: *(Sighs loudly, with vertical shoulder involvement.)* Well, okay, so I didn't turn in my homework today! Do we have to make a federal case out of it?

MR. WORTH: I'm less concerned with your homework being late, although that is an issue. The bigger problem here is that you lied about turning it in. Did you think I wouldn't find out you had lied?

DAISY: I don't know, you put me on the spot, and I had to say something!

Working While Autistic

MR. WORTH: When you have to say something, make it the truth. Honesty is an important aspect of work ethic, which is vital to the Workability experience. You may bring your homework tomorrow and lose the standard 5 points, or bring it to me before 4:00 this afternoon and lose 2.5 points, as stated in the course agreement. And now you may sit down so we can get started.

NARRATOR: *Daunted Daisy slunk back to her seat, her face blazing like the Everburning Fires of Mount Hottenov. She vowed to herself that she would never again lie about turning in her homework, or anything else. As a chaotic good dwarf, dishonesty was deplorable, and she would not tolerate it in her quest for truth and justice.*

ZACH

Because he was the assistant with the least seniority and just a part-timer at the assisted living facility, Zach always got the worst assignments and the dirtiest jobs. He thought he was better than this and shouldn't have to do this kind of menial work that nobody else wanted to do. Then he realized that this was his role, to do the jobs no one else wanted to do, because they had to be done. That's why they hired him in the first place. He decided that the best way for him to deal with this reality was to do the

— Chapter 6 —

best job he could, even on the worst assignments. When there was a mess to be cleaned up and he was instructed to take care of it, he said, "Right away, I'm on it!" and got to work immediately. Then he made sure that everything shone when he was done. He decided to be just as kind to the angriest and crankiest patients as he was to the sweet ones. Maybe even more so. If they were that negative about everything in their world, they probably needed someone to listen to them. Rather than brushing them off to get out of their room as soon as possible, Zach took the time to smile and chat for a minute or two before going on about his business. Paying attention to details, whether it was cleaning up or listening to people, was important. The more he did it, the better he felt about his work there. Doing even the most menial, dirty jobs with the utmost care and treating each person as if they were important brought a level of excellence to Zach's work. He looked forward to going to work every day. Doing the best job he could made him feel like he made a difference.

TRISH

The paper in the copy room was getting low. Trish had been eyeing it for some time. What happened when they ran out? How could they print anything with no paper? A few times she'd commented, to no one in particular, "Hm. It looks like we might need more printer paper at some point." No one said anything. Maybe they didn't hear her; she did have a quiet voice. Maybe they didn't know who she was talking to. For whatever reason, the paper kept getting lower and lower.

Working While Autistic

Finally she realized that just talking generally about a potential problem didn't work. She would have to find out what she could do. She gathered her courage and tapped on her supervisor's half-open door.

"Um, excuse me?"

"Yes, Trish, come on in. How do you like your new job? No problems, I hope?"

"Oh, I love my job!" Trish said quickly, then hesitated. It sounded like her supervisor didn't want to hear about problems, but running out of paper was a problem. What could she say that wouldn't sound like a complaint? She thought about it.

"Trish? Are you okay? You kind of zoned out there for a minute."

"Oh, sorry! I was just thinking." She paused again.

"Yes?"

Trish realized she should come at this problem with a potential solution, and not dump it on her supervisor's desk.

"I was just wondering if I should order new printer paper, or if someone else does that. I noticed it was low, and I'd be happy to order more if someone sends me a link and instructions."

"I'm glad you reminded me! Polly, who usually orders our office supplies, had to take early maternity leave, and I haven't tapped anyone in yet to do the ordering. Dorothea at the front desk can give you all the particulars to order the paper. This will help a lot, thank you!"

Trish was happy to take on that duty while Polly was gone. She was glad that she had been solution focused with her supervisor, not problem focused. Offering to order paper as a solution, rather

– Chapter 6 –

than complaining that they were running out of paper, demonstrated her work ethic.

BILL

Bill jerked awake. Someone had rapped loudly on his car's window.

"Hey, wake up! You're going to be late back from lunch!" Ned, one of his coworkers, was grinning at him. He seemed to enjoy Bill's jumpy overreaction.

"Yeah, I know, I'll be right there." Bill had eaten lunch in his car to get away from all the sensory and social stimulation in the office. After eating, he had closed his eyes for a moment to self-regulate. Now he was going to be late if he didn't hurry.

"You must have had some night last night!" Ned grinned knowingly. "Still hungover?"

"No, nothing like that." Bill got out of the car and brushed off the crumbs from his sandwich. "I was just resting my eyes for a minute."

"Yeah, and snoring like a bulldog with apnea." Ned laughed.

"I guess I must have dozed off for a minute there." Bill felt his face grow warm with embarrassment. He always had an alarm set to give himself time to get back to his desk after lunch. Why hadn't he heard it? Ned carried on a "man-alogue" while they walked to the office, which was fine with Bill. He didn't enjoy small talk, and Ned didn't seem to notice or care that the conversation was one-sided. All Bill could think of was how irresponsible he had been. He would need more self-discipline if he didn't want to get fired for sleeping on the job.

Working While Autistic

After he got to his desk, Bill checked his phone reminders. Yes, there was his after-lunch reminder. It had gone off, but he hadn't noticed it. There were also eight other waiting texts, emails, and reminders that had probably been going off throughout lunch. Had he tuned them all out? That would be different. Usually Bill couldn't tune out any small sound. He realized that he used the same ringtone for incoming texts, emails, calendar appointments, and reminders. When everything sounded the same, the one that was supposed to wake him up after lunch failed to stand out.

That night when he got home, Bill listened to all of the ringtones that were available on his phone. He finally found one that would stand out and catch his attention, without being aversive: the sound of the original *Star Trek* Enterprise Transport Energizer. That really brought back memories; when he closed his eyes, he could almost see Scotty at the controls. Bill set his after-lunch reminder for daily, Monday through Friday, with the new ringtone. As soon as he heard it, he would immediately go back to the office and be ready to work. This discipline would help him to be a more responsible employee, which is what Bill wanted. It would also remind him of a particular passion of his, which always made him happy.

MARIA

Maria had an excellent work ethic, intrinsically. This could have come from her Catholic upbringing with a mother who stressed the importance of obedience and respecting her elders, and a father who valued sticking with a job until it was done. It could

— Chapter 6 —

have come from her autistic features of attention to detail and perfectionism. Whatever the reason, she had no difficulty at all with most of the aspects of work ethic.

Except when it came to communication. She often found herself temporarily mute, unable to put her thoughts into words during staff meetings. She sat silently and hoped no one would ask her a question. Most of the time, her twin strategies of avoiding eye contact and trying to become invisible at the meeting table were effective, but on rare occasions someone would ask her something. She knew they wanted her to feel included, which was a kindness on their part but stressful for her.

Maria decided to create simple scripts to use on these occasions. She thought back to the kinds of questions that had been directed toward her in the past and realized that they were generally versions of, "How are you doing?" and, "Any questions?" She thought about what she could say, something she could practice in advance and deliver at the right time. The phrases she chose were, "Everything's fine with me, thank you," and, "No, no questions, everything's fine." She practiced these out loud to one of her stuffed sloths, an excellent listener, while she imagined herself as a giant robot, impervious and unafraid.

She tried it out at the next staff meeting and was relieved that no one seemed to realize she was just quoting memorized responses. Her scripts fit the kinds of questions that were usually asked, so she felt prepared. Her communication challenge was solved through scripting.

Working While Autistic

ROBERT

Robert was embarrassed that he couldn't remember his boss's name, and it was far too late to ask. He had it on a card stuffed somewhere in his billfold, but it was easier to just call him "Boss." The boss didn't seem to mind.

"Hey, I've got something new for you."

"Sure thing, Boss. Just leave it on the table, and I'll get to it when I finish this radio."

"No, I'll finish the radio. I need you on this one. A guy found their old black-and-white TV in the attic, and he wants to get it fixed up and give it to his brother for a retirement gift."

"No problem, I'll get to it after I finish this."

"You're not hearing me. This one has a deadline. I'll finish the radio, but I need you on the TV. It's important."

Robert felt his shoulders tense. It was hard for him to stop a job in the middle, and almost impossible to let anyone else finish a job that he had started. This was not going to work. He took a deep breath.

"I told you, I can finish both projects. As soon as this radio is done, I'll take care of the TV. Trust me, I can do it."

The boss walked over to his workbench, picked up the radio, and moved it to another table. Then he sat down on a stool beside Robert.

"There are three things you need to know about working here. Number one: I'm the boss. Number two: We are a team. Number three: When number two breaks down, revert to number one. When I tell you I'll finish the radio, you gotta let me finish the

— Chapter 6 —

radio. When I tell you I need you on the TV, then you work on the TV. That's how this works. Got it?"

Robert took a couple of breaths and felt calmer. "You're right, Boss. I just really hate to stop a project in the middle. It's hard for me."

"Yeah, well, we do hard stuff here. No place for wimps, and I know you're no wimp, or I wouldn't have hired you. The TV is on the front counter, and he needs it by Wednesday."

"I'm on it, Boss. You can count on me."

Robert had been retired long enough that he was out of practice working for someone else. He liked to be in charge of his own stuff, not bossed around. He'd thought of this as kind of like the diner, hanging out with the geezers. Even though he felt comfortable here, that didn't mean that he shouldn't respect authority by doing what the boss said. He'd be a good team player if he did what the boss said, even if he had a better idea. It wasn't easy, but it was part of working at a job instead of being retired. He could do this.

MESSAGES FROM AUTISTIC MENTORS

"Be honest about your strengths and weaknesses. If you take on tasks that are not within your strengths, it's not good. I pick something with low small talk and low employee banter. I give myself more breathing room to be good at what I'm good at; otherwise, I'd be anxious."

— Helena, works with autistic children

Working While Autistic

"First of all, the best way to have good work ethic is to make sure you understand the training. You need to know the expectations company-wide, and stick with it. Also, don't leave money on the counter; it's important to take care of it and put it in the cash register right away."

— Suzanne, drive-through window greeter

"Work ethic needs communication, to be able to represent yourself and to work as a team. This is sometimes a challenge for an autist who needs their space and is happy to be alone. It's good to be able to communicate with coworkers about those needs. I have PTSD, so I practice calm to maintain my equilibrium and focus on the task at hand and stay grounded in myself."

— Beth F. Watzke autistic writer and animal care provider

– CHAPTER 7 –
Your Rights
Accommodations & Advocacy

"Equal rights, fair play, justice, are all like the air: we all have it, or none of us has it."
— *Maya Angelou*

"I took breaks and defended my free time fiercely. I taught myself, slowly, that I deserved to be comfortable, relaxed, and happy."
— *Devon Price, PhD*

All disabled employees in the US have rights under the Americans with Disabilities Act (ADA). But are you disabled? If you're not blind, deaf, or intellectually disabled and you don't use a wheelchair, you probably don't look disabled, and you may not feel disabled either. Autism is technically a disability, but it is a brain difference. There's nothing wrong with your autistic brain. When you try to cope with a neuro-majority world that doesn't make accommodations for your sensory and social differences, you might feel disabled. Of course, you don't

Working While Autistic

have to "look disabled" to be eligible for accommodations that will make it easier for you to be productive. But if no one knows you're disabled, you may not get the support you need and deserve.

SHOULD YOU DISCLOSE YOUR DISABILITY?

This is an important question, and one that only you can answer for yourself. However, think carefully before you do so. What are the potential ramifications and benefits if you disclose your autism?

If you have a career in social work or education and work with disabled students or families, it could potentially be a benefit to disclose that you, too, have a disability. Your employer should see that you will relate and work effectively with a neurodivergent population because of your own neurodiversity. In tech and engineering industries, many employers already value the strengths that autistic employees have to offer, such as attention to detail. Of course, every employer is different, and each person must make their own choice whether or not to disclose their autism.

In other career paths, your potential employer may not understand what autism is, and they may have erroneous beliefs that could prejudice them against hiring an autistic employee. This is unfortunate, and I hope that these attitudes will change over time, but realistically, you may meet people in business who hold outdated attitudes.

Does this mean you can't ask for and expect reasonable accommodations? No, I don't think so. You may choose to disclose selected

— Chapter 7 —

things about yourself and ways that simple accommodations can help you to do your best work. Don't expect your boss to make widespread, expensive changes to the workplace to accommodate you, but do have a solution-focused approach.

For example, you might disclose to an employer that you have auditory sensitivity and that sound levels in the office adversely affect the quality of your work. Rather than demanding your own soundproofed office when your coworkers have cubicles or share a workspace, offer to bring your own noise-canceling headphones or earbuds. Let them know that you won't listen to music, the ballgame, or podcasts at work, but that the ear protectors can allow you to focus on your job without distractions.

Here's another example: fluorescent lights. It might seem unrealistic to demand that your employer replace all of the existing ceiling light fixtures. If you have your own office without shared overhead lighting, consider bringing in floor and table lamps of your own choosing, if that's something you would enjoy. However, if your light sensitivity and the distractions of the fluorescent lights impair your ability to do your best work, don't give up on expecting your employer to make changes. They might be willing to replace fluorescent tubes with LED bulbs that fit the same ceiling fixtures.

LED lighting is better for the environment and is actually less expensive and more energy efficient than fluorescent lighting. It would be in the company's best interest to switch out all of their fluorescent tube light bulbs for LED tubes. You'd be doing them a favor to point this out respectfully.

Working While Autistic

Don't get me wrong. I believe you deserve all the accommodations. If it were up to me, every workplace would make all the changes you need, and employers wouldn't think twice about the dollar cost when it comes to their employees' needs. The sad truth, though, is if they can hire someone else who does not ask for a lot of expensive changes to accommodate them, they might go with that person, and miss out on what an amazing employee you would be.

HOW MUCH SHOULD YOU DISCLOSE?

Consider starting small and disclose only the aspects of your autism that most affect your productivity. If being in a busy office is exhausting for you, working from home could be your ideal solution. It's important to demonstrate, if possible, your level of productivity from home. They need to know that you can complete all of the tasks from home that you would have completed in the office. A hybrid option, working from home on some days and in the office on other days, may be an acceptable solution. Depending on your place of work, they may require that you disclose your autism with a diagnostic letter and recommendation before they allow you to work from home. There's never a guarantee, but it can be worth it if it lets you avoid the hectic office as much as possible.

– Chapter 7 –

WHO SHOULD YOU TELL?

If you want special accommodations, then you will probably need to disclose your reason for the request to Human Resources in a large business, or to your boss or supervisor in a small or family company. You decide whether you disclose your autism diagnosis, or specific characteristics, such as sound or light sensitivity. What you share with management or HR is confidential. Unless you really know all of your coworkers well and have relationships with them outside of work, you might not want to share your diagnosis with everyone. It's difficult to know how they might respond, and it's possible that they will treat you differently.

WHAT ARE REASONABLE ACCOMMODATIONS?

What's reasonable varies, but it's important to focus on the aspects of the workplace that are the most problematic for your own productivity, and the ones which will be most cost-effective for your employers.

Some reasonable accommodations for disabilities include making the workplace accessible, such as ramps for wheelchairs, restructured job descriptions or modified work schedules, and specialized, accessible equipment. Reasonable accommodations for autistic employees might include alternative lighting, assigning a job coach or mentor, noise-canceling headsets, sensory breaks, visual cues, working from home for part or all of your work week, and a flexible schedule with reduced hours. A shorter work week may increase your productivity by reducing stress. Devon Price wrote, "Research on productivity, burnout, and mental health all suggest that the average workday is far too long, and ... not sustainable for most people." Joe Sanok, author of *Thursday is the New Friday*, writes, "The four-day workweek is already here. We are the post-pandemic generation that will reshape how we look at work." I hope you create a work schedule that supports you with time to rest from your labors and enjoy your other passions outside of work.

Every workplace is different, of course, and there is no guarantee that you will be given every accommodation you request. Still, it's important to advocate for what you need, with an emphasis on the fact that these accommodations will make you a more productive employee.

KNOW YOUR RIGHTS, BUT AVOID FIGHTS

Your rights under ADA prevent discrimination against qualified individuals with disabilities. While the ADA requires that the employer make reasonable accommodations, such as those listed above, this is only required if it does not place an "undue hardship" on the business. A small business might be friendly and willing to accommodate, but unable to afford big changes. A large company may have more financial ability to accommodate, but it may also be less personal and less willing to accommodate one employee

– Chapter 7 –

when they have hundreds who do not need accommodations. This is unfortunate, but it can be true for some companies.

If you make demands on day one and expect them to change the entire office to accommodate you, you will probably meet with resistance. It's better not to battle with your boss. Yes, you could bring in a lawyer and force them to make accommodations because you know your rights, but this seldom ends well. You may not keep that job for long if you are seen as a "troublemaker," and you may have difficulty finding another job without a good reference. It is better to work with them, rather than position yourself against them, for the greater good of the company and your own future.

CUPS

If you're not sure how much to disclose, or to whom, use the CUPS acronym from *Independent Living While Autistic*. CUPS stands for *closeness*, *understanding*, *professionalism*, and *support*.

Closeness

The C in CUPS stands for *closeness*.

If you're close to someone, you may want to disclose that you're autistic. At work, closeness is not simply someone whose cubicle happens to be near yours, or who you eat lunch with every day at work. A close work friend is someone you also socialize with outside of work. If you have each other's personal phone numbers, text each other, and make plans to do things together on weekends, that person is a closer friend than your other colleagues.

Understanding

The U in CUPS is for *understanding*.

Sometimes you may find that people have trouble understanding you or why you do things the way you do. If you feel that your working relationship will be better if they understand that you are neurodivergent, consider sharing, at least to some extent. You may choose to say something like, "I'm autistic. That's why I can't talk on the phone when someone else is talking in the same room," or something like, "I'm the kind of person who has auditory processing issues, so regular conversation levels can affect me more than most people." If they really need to understand you better, you decide how much to disclose.

Professionalism

The P in CUPS is for *professionalism*.

Disclosing your autism to your HR department is disclosure for professional reasons. It's still up to you to decide how much to disclose in order to get your needs met.

Support

The S in CUPS is for *support*.

The more support you need in the way of work accommodations, the more you will need to disclose to HR or your boss. If you

— Chapter 7 —

want them to make big changes, they need to know that this is an actual disability, not just a preference on your part.

Let's see how our six characters in search of employment coped with workplace rights and accommodations.

SIX CHARACTERS IN SEARCH OF EMPLOYMENT

DAISY

NARRATOR: *Once more, the sound of the coffee grinder on the espresso machine startles our hero, Peridot Goldhammer the Mighty, as she attempts to answer a customer's question about where to find tulip bulbs. Her sensitive startle reflex kicks in, and she finds herself temporarily unable to use spoken words effectively. Finally, she points to the aisle with spring bulbs and retreats to the break room to recover. Upon her return, she approaches Lilac.*

DAISY: Lilac, I'm sorry, but you're going to have to get a new espresso machine. This one is terrible!

LILAC: What are you talking about? It's nearly new, and I have had zero complaints about it.

DAISY: Well, I'm complaining now. The grinder is too loud. It startles me, and then I can't do my

Working While Autistic

DAISY: job. I just can't stand another day of this, so
(continued) it's going to have to go. You know, because I'm autistic and the ADA gives me rights.

LILAC: I see. Well, I'll miss you, Daisy. I've really enjoyed having you here. I think you have a lot of potential in this work.

DAISY: But I don't want to go.

LILAC: Well, you told me you can't do your job and that you can't stand another day.

DAISY: I won't have to leave if you just buy a quiet espresso machine.

LILAC: A new machine is out of the question. This is an expensive, restaurant-quality piece of equipment, and I'm pretty sure they all make the same sound when they grind the coffee beans.

DAISY: But the ADA means you have to make accommodations for disabled employees. That's me.

LILAC: I know about the ADA. It says, "reasonable accommodations." And you're a Workability student, not a full employee. Even if you were, this issue shows that this is not the right job for you. It's best if you find a career path that

— Chapter 7 —

LILAC: suits you now, while you're young, rather than wasting your time here if you can't stand it.
(continued)

DAISY: But I love working here!

LILAC: And I love having you work here. But what can we do?

NARRATOR: *Our hero put on her thinking helmet.*

DAISY: Well, how about if I wear ear protectors while I'm working?

LILAC: That could work. What kind of ear protectors?

DAISY: I have some ear plugs that let in most sounds, like people talking, but they kind of filter out the loudest sounds. I wear them at the movies because the volume is too high for me, but I want to hear the dialogue.

LILAC: Sure, you could wear those at work. Will that help?

DAISY: I think it will.

LILAC: Wonderful! I didn't want to lose you, Daisy.

Daisy learned that her rights under the ADA didn't mean that she could dictate expensive changes to her workplace and automatically get whatever she asked for, but that she could ask for and receive reasonable accommodations. Her earplugs allowed her to hear customers but softened the shock of the espresso machine. Later, when she was trained as a barista, she found that turning the grinder off and on several times helped her get used to the noise in a way that she could control. She was grateful that Lilac understood even though she couldn't afford to buy a new machine, and that she was welcomed, and even appreciated, as a worker.

ZACH

Zach closed his eyes. He was supposed to do three things before he clocked out, but he only remembered two of them. He sat in the staff room at the assisted living facility. The manager, Martin, had just left. He had told Zach three things that he had to do, and then he asked if Zach had any special plans for the weekend, talked about his weekend trip to see his parents, and left. Now, Zach couldn't remember the third thing Martin told him to do. He remembered that he was supposed to clean up the art materials in the recreation room and disinfect the surfaces in the kitchen, but what was the third thing? While he did the two tasks he remembered, he racked his brain to try to remember the other one.

Zach had always struggled with auditory memory. If someone wrote down what he was supposed to do, no problem, but if they told him verbally? Big problem. He used to take notes when a teacher or supervisor told him anything verbally. When Martin went straight from telling him three things to do to engaging in a social conversation about the weekend, it threw him for a loop.

— Chapter 7 —

He knew it would be rude to take notes while Martin chatted with him. It was stressful to maintain orientation toward him with an appropriate attentive facial expression until he was done, and now it was too late. His memory could only hold two of the things.

When he finished the jobs he remembered, he sat down and worried. Should he text Martin? They all had his number to text in emergencies, but was this an emergency? Zach decided that if the thing he forgot was something important to do for a client, it would be bad if he didn't do it, so he texted Martin.

Luckily, Martin responded right away. The third thing was to tell Mr. Swanson that his daughter would be visiting him tomorrow afternoon. Martin thanked him and went to take care of it. Mr. Swanson was delighted to hear about the upcoming visit, and Zach was glad to be able to give him happy news before he left for the day.

Monday morning Martin called Zach in and asked him why he had texted him about such a minor thing on a Friday evening. Zach took a deep breath and thought about how to answer.

"I have a problem remembering what I hear. I can't seem to hold it in my memory if I can't see it. Usually I make notes as soon as you tell me what to do, but we got to chatting about the weekend, and by the time I went to write it down, I could only remember two of the things I was supposed to do. I am really sorry."

"I didn't realize you had an auditory problem. How can I help?"

"The best thing for me would be if you could write down what I'm supposed to do, instead of just telling me. It could be a text, email, or sticky note. As long as I can see it, I can do it."

Working While Autistic

"No problem, Zach. I'll do that from now on. In fact, I should probably be doing that with everyone, not only you. Thanks for the idea."

Zach was relieved that Martin wasn't upset about it. He had wondered if he would have to tell him about his autism, but it wasn't needed. Maybe one day he would, as it seemed Martin was pretty open, but not today. He was able to get the accommodation he needed without disclosing a disability.

TRISH

Trish put her head down on her desk and closed her eyes. The hum of the overhead fluorescent lights, along with the rapid flickering, worked together to give her a monster headache. No matter how she tried, she could not tune out the distractions, and by the end of the day, she was exhausted and unable to focus on even the simplest of tasks. The laminate of her desk felt cool on her forehead, and she breathed slowly, seeking calm.

"Trish, are you okay?"

She jumped and sat up quickly. Her supervisor, Stacie, stood by her desk with a concerned look on her face.

"Oh! I-I'm sorry! I'll get right back to work," she stammered.

"Don't worry about that. I just wanted to know if you're okay."

"I'm okay." Trish blinked hard several times and rubbed her temples.

"You don't look okay. Tell me what's wrong. I'm sure we can fix it."

— Chapter 7 —

Trish wasn't sure how much she should tell Stacie. Being bothered by lights sounded so weak and lame. What should she say? The silence went on too long, and Stacie pulled up a chair and sat down.

"Trish, I want to help you so you can do your job. I understand you might need accommodations."

"Accommodations? What for?"

"Whatever you need. Remember when you started your internship here?"

"Of course." Trish had been thrilled to get the assignment her senior year.

"Your application came through the disabled student services. You disclosed on your application to us that you're autistic."

"Oh yeah, I had forgotten. Is that a problem now that I'm not a student intern anymore?"

"Not at all. We know what a good worker you are. But you have rights as an employee with a disability, and if we can help make your job easier for you, let us know."

Trish didn't know what to say. "Thank you," she finally murmured.

"So why don't you tell me why you've been sitting here with your head on your desk. What's the problem?"

"Well, since you asked, the overhead lights are so loud and flickery, it makes my head ache, so it's hard for me to concentrate."

Stacie looked up. "They make a noise and flicker? I don't hear or see anything."

"You're right, It's probably nothing. I'll get used to it."

Working While Autistic

"That's not what I meant. You shouldn't have to put up with headaches to work here. What kind of light would be better?"

"Anything but fluorescent. But you can't replace all the lights in the office for one person." Trish felt embarrassed to have disclosed her problem with the lights, since she didn't see any solution for it.

"You're probably right. We may not be able to replace all the lights, but your corner here is on a separate switch. We can turn off your overhead lights and keep the rest of them on in the other offices."

"Hmm ..." Trish didn't want to point out that she couldn't read files in the dark. Stacie was trying so hard to be helpful, and she didn't want to appear ungrateful.

"Of course, you'll need other lighting instead." Stacie looked around. "Oh, I know. When they redecorated the freshman dorm, they replaced all the lamps with overhead lighting. There are some floor lamps and desk lamps in storage that no one's using. They're ancient, but sturdy. I'm sure we can find a couple that still work."

"That would be wonderful!" Trish's eyes filled with tears. She was touched by how much trouble Stacie was going to on her behalf. "Thank you so much." She looked down and blinked away her tears before they could fall.

"Don't worry about a thing, Trish. We love having you here full-time now, and if there's anything else you need, please let me know."

It turned out that the old dorm lamps were not sufficient or reliable, but that didn't stop Stacie. She did some research and found that they could replace the overhead fluorescent tubes with

— Chapter 7 —

LED bulbs, which fit the same fixtures, were cheaper, lasted longer, and were better for the environment. If it hadn't been for Trish, she would not have discovered this solution that was better for everyone, including the college budget.

Trish had not thought to ask for accommodations in her job; she just tried to tough it out. Fortunately, she didn't need to disclose her disability because she had already done so as an intern. Her supervisor helped her get the accommodations she deserved, even though she didn't ask. Trish realized what a rarity this was in the world, and she was grateful all over again for her good fortune.

BILL

Bill had been at his new job for a few months when the pandemic hit, and everyone transitioned to working from home. Bill loved it! Of course, he hated the reason for it, but not having to go into the office, hear his coworkers on their phones, smell their lunches in the staff room microwave, and endure random social conversations was wonderful. Suddenly, he became much more productive. He completed his regular tasks halfway through the day and asked for more work. His supervisor loved it and sent him as much extra work as he could handle, which was a lot. He even got a promotion and a modest raise while working from home.

Then the day came when everyone returned to the office. On his first day, Bill heard the happy, excited voices of people as they reconnected, caught up, and agreed how glad they were to be back. Working from home was not, apparently, as successful for everyone else as it had been for Bill. He struggled to cope with the sensory

Working While Autistic

and social aspects of the office, but after a few months away from it, it seemed to affect him more and more. He could barely think by noon, and he dragged his feet coming back in after lunch every day, even with his phone reminders.

One day Mr. Brisbee called him into his office, and he looked serious.

"Bill, I don't know what's going on with you these days. Problems at home?"

"Problems at home? No, not at all. Why do you ask?"

"Your productivity has really gone downhill. You were our top worker for several months in a row, and suddenly you're at the bottom. If you've got a problem with alcohol or other substances, we can recommend a program. You can kick this, Bill, I know you can. You're too valuable an employee to let addictions get in the way of your future."

"Addictions? I'm not an alcoholic or a drug user. Why would you think that?"

"Well, usually when someone's work declines so rapidly and they take long breaks and avoid people at work, there's some kind of addiction involved. Help is available, Bill, you just need to admit that you have a problem."

"No, it's nothing like that! I'm not an addict, I'm autistic!" He had blurted it out without thinking, and now he wondered if he had made a mistake.

"Autistic? Well, why didn't you say so? You're not the only one, you know. So, tell me, what accommodation do you need to get

— Chapter 7 —

you back up to speed? I know you can do a great job, but I don't see it right now."

"Everything was perfect when I worked from home. No distractions, no social chit-chat, no sensory issues. I could really focus on my job. I loved it. I wish I could keep working from home now that the lockdown is over."

"Well, let me talk to HR about that. Because you have a documentable track record of increased productivity from home and decreased productivity in the office, I think I can make a case for you. They worry that people who work from home will goof off, but clearly that's not the case for you."

"Thank you, Mr. Brisbee! That would be amazing!"

HR did approve the request, after receiving a diagnostic letter from Bill's doctor stating that he was autistic. Bill couldn't have been happier with the new arrangement. Even though he hadn't planned to disclose his autism at work, it seemed like the right thing to do in the moment, and he was glad he had told his boss that he was autistic. Working from home was the perfect accommodation for Bill.

MARIA

Maria's phone buzzed, and she jumped. She drew back and stared at it as if it were a harpy eagle, predator and enemy of sloths. Should she pick it up? She didn't want to talk to anyone. If she left it alone, how soon would it stop that annoying rattle on the table with each vibration? If she picked it up to silence it, would

Working While Autistic

she touch the wrong button and answer it by mistake? While she considered her options, it stopped, finally.

After a short break to regain her composure, Maria checked her message. It was work. They had a new manuscript for her to proof, and they had emailed it to her. Then why call? It seemed cruel to add this stressor to what should have been an enjoyable task. She loved proofreading new books, so when she saw a new one in her inbox, she always felt a special joy. She was needed! But why spoil it all by calling her on the telephone, of all things? The telephone! How she hated it! She watched a few minutes of Sloth TV and felt calmer.

When she reviewed her phone messages, she saw that all of the voicemail messages came from Tillie, one of her colleagues. The other two emailed her what they wanted her to do, but not Tillie. Apparently, Tillie loved the telephone, couldn't get enough of it. She just had to call when an email would have sufficed. Although Maria had figured out how to silence her phone, it still vibrated loudly with each ring. Perhaps when the twins were home, they could help her make that stop too.

For now, though, Maria had a problem. How could she get Tillie to stop calling her on the phone? She thought about it, and then wrote a draft of an email she might send. It said, "Tillie, thank you for phoning me about the manuscript for me to proof. I will be happy to get started on it right away. In the future, it will be helpful for me if you would email me instead of telephoning me about new manuscripts. I am much more productive in print

— Chapter 7 —

than I am on the phone. The sound of my phone vibrating is the absolute worst sound in the world, and I hate it!"

She emailed her friend, Sofia, and asked her if she would review the message before she sent it to Tillie. Sofia was so good at looking at things from both sides. Sofia said it was mostly fine, and that she certainly had the right to ask for this simple change, but that she should delete the last sentence about the sound of her phone, and add another thank-you sentence at the end. Maria made the necessary changes and sent it to Tillie.

What a relief when Tillie replied, "Sure, no problem!" What seemed like a huge issue was handled with one email. Maria was grateful that Sofia had helped her soften the edges of her request, and that Tillie had been so agreeable about it. Accommodation granted; problem solved!

ROBERT

"Excuse me, Boss." Robert ducked out the back door. The boss was chatting with the man who came in to pick up the refurbished TV from his childhood as a gift for his brother. They laughed and brought up old TV shows they had loved back in the day. It was too much for Robert, so he was out of there. He walked around the block, peeked in the window, and then walked around the block again because they were still yammering away in there. He couldn't focus on his work with all that was going on. Finally, after four times around the block, they were gone, and he slunk back in.

"That was a mighty long break," Guy said.

Working While Autistic

"Sorry, Boss." Robert sat down at the workbench and picked up one of his tools, ready to get back to work.

"You know, I saw you going by. Why didn't you come back inside? How long of a break do you need, anyway?"

Robert put down his tool and sighed. What could he say? He didn't want the boss to think he was a work shirker. "I don't usually need such a long break," he said.

"I didn't think so. So what gives?"

"I'm just not good with social stuff. All that chit-chat and laughing about stuff, it drives me up a wall sometimes. I have to get away and be alone for a while before I can get my head back on straight."

"You and I are always chatting and laughing about one thing or another, and you never bailed on me before. Why now?"

"Well, I know you. I'm comfortable talking with you, one-on-one like this, but when we get a group of people I don't know gabbing, I just have to leave."

"Since when is one talkative customer a 'group'? I don't get it."

Robert wondered what he should say. If he said he was autistic, would the boss think he was damaged goods? Would he fire him? He didn't want to lose this job.

"I guess I'm one of those geezers who's uncomfortable with social stuff, like chatting with people I don't know."

"Well, that's okay, Robert. Chatting is not part of your job description, but working is. If you take a break every time a customer comes in, I don't see how you'll get your work done."

Chapter 7

"Oh, I can do my work. Don't you worry about that! Usually I stay and keep working while you do the whole customer service thing. It was just today, when it went on so long, and he had that annoying laugh ..."

"Oh, yeah, the snort-laugh! That was a hoot, wasn't it?" Guy chuckled.

"It grated on my nerves. I'll make you a deal, Boss. If you don't get mad when I take an extra break to get away from things for a while, I promise you I will get the job done before I leave. I know I can do it."

"Yeah, I know you can do it too. I won't worry about your breaks, if you keep doing the work the way you have been. You do that, and I'll handle the front-desk customers, even the snort laughers."

The two of them had another chuckle at that. Robert was relieved that he could take a break if he needed it, when the social stress got to be too much. He hadn't had to tell his boss about his autism, but maybe someday he would.

MESSAGES FROM AUTISTIC MENTORS

Disclosing a Diagnosis:

"I chose not to disclose my diagnosis; I didn't feel like it was information that would benefit my employer or me to have it known. I did disclose my child's diagnosis as a reference for working with autistic children in schools."

— Helena, works with autistic children

Working While Autistic

"I've been told that I should tell corporate that I'm autistic, but I don't want to have to prove my autism. I'd rather make accommodations with the manager at my site, such as having a mat on the floor to stand on, and sometimes turning the overhead fan off. You can ask for accommodations without filing official disability documentation if you'd rather do it that way."

— Suzanne, drive-through window greeter

"We need accommodations and a way to ask for them without jeopardizing our chance of being hired. My fear is that if I don't disclose my disability and later ask for the accommodations, that might be breaking the law, but if I do disclose, I might not get the job, because they can hire someone else who does not need accommodations. It's complicated. It would be good to have a script for how to ask for accommodations."

— Beth F. Watzke, late-diagnosed autistic writer and animal care provider

Sensory Strategies:

"Work is overstimulating. When I get home from work, I spend ten to fifteen minutes with my eyes closed under my weighted blanket with the lights low and a sound machine, to settle down before transitioning between working and home."

— Helena, works with autistic children

— Chapter 7 —

"I'm mostly sensitive to sounds. For me, working at the window means staying away from the blenders and coffee grinders. If there's a lot of noise, I want to be close to a window."

— Suzanne, drive-through window greeter

"I make sure I have water, snack foods, and I wear clothing that is comfortable, or I will get distracted. I meditate to be in a good positive place for self-energy. Deep breathing helps me stay present and take care of myself so I can do the job."

— Beth F. Watzke, late-diagnosed autistic writer and animal care provider

Social Overload Strategies:

"I just smile and nod and ask people questions about themselves, because people like to talk about themselves. If I can get other people to talk about themselves, then all I have to think of are questions to ask."

— Helena, works with autistic children

"Socially, I do not want to be micro-managed. I don't want anyone touching my computer or reaching over me to get something without asking me or letting me know. It's better for me if they just ask for something instead of just reaching into my space to get it. I don't like a lot of hands in my personal space, so I tell them. I've had to say, 'Please don't touch my computer,' to people I've worked with."

— Suzanne, drive-through window greeter

Working While Autistic

"When I was a smoker, that was my excuse to step outside and get away. I'll still step outside if I need to. Meditation helps."
— Beth F. Watzke, late-diagnosed autistic writer and animal care provider

CHAPTER 8
Your Kryptonite
Office Politics

"When you hear people making hateful comments, stand up to them. Point out what a waste it is to hate, and you could open their eyes."

— *Taylor Swift*

"You simply cannot tell other people they are stupid, even if they really are stupid."

— *Dr. Temple Grandin*

One of the things many autistic people dread about the workplace is office politics. It's the worst, isn't it? Nobody likes it, but it can be difficult to avoid.

Office politics refers to informal power structures, rather than the obvious, formal ones. The formal power structures can be found on your employer's website, employee handbook, or hierarchy chart. The relationship between managers and the workers they supervise is usually well-understood and straightforward.

Working While Autistic

But there are unspoken rules in the workplace, too, and they can have a big impact on you and your success at work. Office politics is linked to these unspoken rules and expectations. It can take the form of gossip. Sometimes someone tries to win favor with the boss and throws their coworkers under the bus in pursuit of the next promotion or raise. It can even include outright bullying. Most autistic employees prefer things to be clear and fair, so that everyone knows what to expect, rather than shady or changeable. Office politics can affect your ability to do your best work the way Kryptonite weakens Superman. Here are some tips to tackle this monster: use KRYPTONITE to help you remember: *knowledge, respect, yield, professionalism, team, own, notice, ignore, true, enlighten.*

KRYPTONITE

KNOWLEDGE

The K in KRYPTONITE stands for *knowledge*.

Get to know the formal hierarchy of your workplace. Find out who reports to whom and which managers are responsible for which departments. If someone tries to sidestep the accepted power structure, hijack another colleague's project, or pawn off their least favorite tasks onto someone else, you need to know. If someone who is not your manager tries to give you tasks or assignments, taking them on without question can feel like the helpful thing to do. However, expecting you to do their job for them is not okay. When in doubt, write it out. If a colleague who is not your

— Chapter 8 —

boss gives you an assignment, email that person and copy your direct manager. Lay out in the email what you understood about what they asked you to do. Let them know that if you have been assigned a new project, you'd like guidance from your manager on how to prioritize the new task with your existing projects. If your manager thanks you for taking it on or tells you it's a high priority, great. Now you know that you should do it. On the other hand, if your manager does not approve this assignment, they can take it up with your colleague and remind them that they are not the boss of you. But probably with more professional language. In any case, it's not your job to school your colleagues; let management do that. After all, that's why they get paid the middle-sized bucks.

RESPECT

The R in KRYPTONITE stands for *respect*.

Respect in the workplace is the opposite of office politics. When you're respectful, you don't listen to or spread gossip. You don't get pulled into petty disputes among your coworkers, and you don't take sides. You don't eat someone else's yogurt that they left in the break room refrigerator, even if they didn't write their name on it. You know it's not yours, so you keep your hands off of it. That's respectful, and it's a great antidote to the on-the-job nonsense that sometimes goes on in the workplace.

Working While Autistic

YIELD

The Y in KRYPTONITE stands for *yield*.

When you're on the road and you see a yield sign, you know to let the other driver have the right-of-way. Even if there's no sign, you'd rather yield and let someone else go first than insist on your rights and end up in a crash. Yielding at work is important, too If someone says something that you disagree with, ask yourself: Do I want to risk a wreck, or should I yield and let it go? Most of the things that get said around the break room are not earth-shattering, and if you let it go, nothing terrible will happen. If you do insist on your opinion being the right one, what are the odds that you could actually change their mind? Probably slim. At times like that, it's better to yield, let the traffic go by, and stay below the radar of office politics.

PROFESSIONAL

The P in KRYPTONITE stands for *professional*.

It's professional to keep your mind and your conversations work-related when you're at work. I know this seems so obvious, but you may find that you have coworkers who want to discuss all kinds of private matters in public spaces. Ignore them, and politely get back to your work without being drawn into their drama; it's the professional response.

– Chapter 8 –

TEAM

The first T in KRYPTONITE stands for *team*.

It is important to be a team player. You can do this without getting bogged down by office politics. Do your job well. Meet your deadlines so your team members who need your information can get on with their part of the project. Support one another on your team. This doesn't mean you have to be the team "water boy" who does all the extra chores while the self-proclaimed "star players" kick back and take it easy. One way to be a good team player is, if you take the last cup of coffee, make a new pot. If the printer runs out of paper or toner while you're using it, replace it rather than leaving it for the next person to find. That's what a good team member would do. If you're the only woman on your team and your colleagues expect you to always make the coffee and clean the kitchen, that is wrong. You are not their mom or their waitress. You are a team member with equal standing. Everyone on your team, including you, deserves respect.

OWN

The O in KRYPTONITE stands for *own*.

When you have been at fault, own up to your part in the office political scene. Don't try to pass the buck or throw someone else under the bus. Own up to it. If necessary, apologize. The best apologies have three parts.

You can use OWN to remember the three parts of a good apology: own it, Why?, needed changes.

First, *own it* by acknowledging what you did.

Working While Autistic

Second, *Why?* Show that you understand by stating why it was the wrong thing to do.

Third, *needed changes*. Share the changes you need to make to ensure that you don't make the same mistake over and over.

We all make mistakes. Your boss wants to know that you are the kind of employee who learns from your mistakes so that you don't repeat them. Own it.

NOTICE

The N in KRYPTONITE stands for *notice*.

Notice what's going on around the office. If someone has a birthday and you see that there is a card to sign, sign it. Later you can remember and wish that person a happy birthday. However, do take notice of whether or not there is a surprise planned for lunchtime and people secretly sign the card while hiding it from the recipient. In that case, do not tell them happy birthday until after the surprise. If you notice that someone is slacking off, don't tattle to the boss. Just continue to do your job to the best of your ability. Don't display an obvious "holier than thou" attitude, but also don't lower yourself to their standard. You can notice what's going on without copying everything you see. Do the best job you can; it will always be the right choice and may be noticed and appreciated.

— Chapter 8 —

IGNORE

The I in KRYPTONITE stands for *ignore*.

If two of your coworkers seem to be mad at each other, try your best to steer clear of them and ignore it. Whatever you do, do not let them tell you their side of the dispute. That is a messy road, and you do not want to go down it. Having a script prepared, such as, "I understand that there is something going on with you and (other person), but it's really not my business. I appreciate you both as colleagues, so I'll stay out of it." Keep your head down, ignore other people's drama, and do your own work.

TRUE

The second T in KRYPTONITE stands for *true*.

Be true to your ideals and standards. Just because someone else might think it's okay to take a dollar or two from petty cash for the vending machine or take home pens or sticky notes from the supply closet, it doesn't mean you should do the same. You know better, so be true to yourself. If they try to get you to join them in their mini crime spree, it might seem as if they think you're cool like them, but it's probably because they want you to sink to their level. Then, if they get caught, they can say, "Everybody does it."

But, no, everybody doesn't steal from their employer. Theft is theft, even if it is only little things. This doesn't necessarily mean that you are obligated to be a whistleblower, unless it is something you deem to be important enough to report to the boss. If you can look the other way over a pencil or roll of tape, try to stay out of it

Working While Autistic

to minimize drama. It's your call though. The important thing is that your standards are worth upholding. Be true to them.

ENLIGHTEN

The E in KRYPTONITE stands for *enlighten*.

When all else fails, it may be time to enlighten your direct supervisor, manager, or HR to let them know what's going on and to seek their help to solve disputes. Don't go over people's heads, but do enlighten the ones who most need to know.

SIX CHARACTERS IN SEARCH OF EMPLOYMENT

DAISY

NARRATOR: *The absolute worst fate has befallen our hero. One of the chattering, chuckling cheerleaders in Work Study has been assigned to Lilacs & Lattes. Daisy will have to work side by side with her, transforming this oasis of calm into a tornado of drama.*

CAITLIN: Hi, I'm Caitlin. I guess we'll be working together or something.

DAISY: Hi, I guess. I'm Daisy. So, is that Keightlynne, Kaity-Lynn, or Caitlin with a C?

— Chapter 8 —

CAITLIN: With a C, of course. *(sighs deeply)* Look, I'm only here because they didn't have an opening at the boutique, so—*(her phone chimes, she looks at it)* OMG, I have to take this call right now. You don't mind. *(to her cell phone)* It's about time! Did you read my text?

DAISY: Actually, we're not supposed to use our phones—

CAITLIN: *(holds up her hand palm out, then turns away and continues to talk on her phone)*

DAISY: *(louder)* I mean, if you'd rather talk on your phone, I guess this is not the job for you. Off you go, then. Buh-bye.

CAITLIN: *(into her phone)* Just a sec, I have to get rid of this weirdo. *(turns back to Daisy)* That's not for you to say, is it? I need the Work Study credit for my college apps, and Mr. Worth and that Lilac woman both okayed it, so here I am. Deal with it. *(back into the phone)* It's just Crazy Daisy from school. I know, right? Anyway …

NARRATOR: *How will our hero survive? What else does Fate have in store for poor Daisy the Downhearted?*

CAITLIN: *(into her phone)* Of course I'm sure! There were two lines! Two! That means pregnant! I can't

Working While Autistic

CAITLIN: even believe it! What's going to happen to me
(continued) now? My life is ruined!

NARRATOR: *What's this? The chattering cheerleader is pregnant? Perhaps this will bode well for our hero, if Caitlin with a C is forced to drop out to have her baby.*

DAISY: *(approaches Lilac)* Lilac? Can I talk to you in private, please?

LILAC: Of course, Daisy. What is it?

DAISY: Well, I don't know if you're aware, but Caitlin with a C is pregnant, so I assume she's going to drop out. We don't really need her, though, because I can do everything myself.

LILAC: Are you sure? What makes you think she's pregnant?

DAISY: I heard her telling her friend on the phone just now. Which she's not supposed to be using during working hours, so ...

LILAC: Caitlin? Would you come over here, please?

CAITLIN: Sure, I guess. Why?

LILAC: Is there anything you want to tell me about your ... condition?

— Chapter 8 —

CAITLIN: My conditioner? *(tosses her blonde curls)* It's from France. Everyone wants to know where they can get it, but it's very exclusive.

LILAC: No, I meant your ... condition. I understand you're ... pregnant?

CAITLIN: Pregnant?

LILAC: There's nothing to be ashamed of. These things happen. I want you to know that I am here to support you in any way you need.

CAITLIN: I am not pregnant! Who's spreading lies about me?

LILAC: *(glances at Daisy)* Well, someone heard you talking about it on your phone. I know we usually don't allow phone use during your working hours, but I understand that this is a special circumstance.

CAITLIN: That liar! She's such a weirdo. *(turns to Daisy)* Why are you lying about me, you freak? *(back to Lilac)* You can't believe anything Crazy Daisy says!

DAISY: But I heard you tell your friend on the phone. I couldn't help it, your voice is kind of loud, and I have excellent hearing.

Working While Autistic

CAITLIN: I never said I was pregnant!

DAISY: But you said there were two lines on the pregnancy test and your life is ruined.

CAITLIN: My idiot father's stupid girlfriend is pregnant! She did this on purpose to trick him into marrying her. I won't share my daddy with her spawn! They're ruining my life!

LILAC: So ... not pregnant?

CAITLIN: Of course not! This freak is lying about me to try to get me to quit, so she can be the only Work Study student here, but I'm not leaving. Get used to it, weirdo!

LILAC: I think an apology is in order here.

DAISY: I agree. I'm waiting.

CAITLIN: If you think I'm apologizing to you, you're crazier than you look!

DAISY: So you think *I* owe *you* an apology?

LILAC: Daisy, you started a rumor about Caitlin, one that could have harmed her reputation. You are at fault here. Although I don't condone name-calling, this was an upsetting accusation. Daisy, what do you have to say?

— Chapter 8 —

NARRATOR: *Our hero was stunned into silence. She didn't mean to start a rumor; she thought Lilac ought to know if Caitlin was pregnant. But she was wrong. Caitlin wasn't pregnant after all. So that meant Caitlin would not be leaving. They'd be stuck together for the rest of the term. A sobering thought. Daisy ... Has ... No ... Words ...*

LILAC: Daisy, I see you need some time to think about what you want to say. You can gather your thoughts and write a letter of apology. Please bring it to work tomorrow afternoon and we'll meet again.

Daisy had time to think about what she had done. She had jumped to a conclusion based on a conversation she wasn't part of, and then she shared misinformation with Lilac. She had been guilty of potentially starting a rumor. Luckily, no one else had heard, and she knew Lilac would never tell anyone. But Daisy was in the wrong, and she had to own up to her mistake. It was disrespectful to gossip and spread damaging misinformation, and it could have a negative effect on the whole workplace. She wrote a letter saying what she had done and why she realized now that it was wrong. She apologized to both Caitlin and Lilac and promised that in the future, she would not spread rumors or repeat gossip. They accepted her apology. Daisy realized that she'd always thought Caitlin was so stuck up that she would be unaffected by anything

Working While Autistic

Daisy could say, but apparently even cheerleaders had feelings that could be hurt. She was incredibly annoying and entitled, but she deserved respect as much as anyone else. Daisy would not soon forget this lesson.

ZACH

"... Happy birthday to you!" The staff finished singing to Bethany, the receptionist, and she waved an empty file folder to extinguish the candles rather than blowing on the cake. Zach was relieved that everyone on staff was health-conscious and considerate, so no one blew out candles. Martin always brought cake whenever anyone had a birthday. This one was decorated with strawberries and whipped cream, because Martin knew that was Bethany's favorite. This was a great place to work, and Zach appreciated the team spirit, respect, and cooperation that were part of the workplace culture.

While the cake was still being cut, Martin wished Bethany happy birthday again and left for a meeting at one of their sister facilities. Zach noticed that everyone cleaned up their paper plates, threw their trash away, and washed their own coffee cups before they went back to work, so he did the same. It's not like they had a maid on staff to pick up after them. Everyone on this team took care of their own messes.

Later, when he came by the staff room for his next break, Zach noticed that the cake was still out on the table. He worried about the whipped cream and strawberries at room temperature all day. Who was supposed to put it away? Martin brought it, but he was

— Chapter 8 —

gone. It was for Bethany, but she shouldn't have to clean up after her own birthday. Zach realized that no one was responsible for this job. It was a new experience. Should he tell someone the cake was still out? Thinking that through made him realize that it would sound childish. Someone should clean it up, and he was someone. He looked through the drawers in the kitchenette and found a roll of plastic wrap. He covered the cake, moved a few things to make room in the fridge, and slid it onto a shelf. Zach felt good about taking care of a job that he noticed needed to be done without asking for help. He was part of the team, and that was important.

TRISH

"Why won't you come with us? You're too young to be such a stick-in-the-mud." Steph checked her lipstick using her phone camera, and then took a quick selfie.

"You never come with us. You should try having fun sometime. You might like it," added Chelsea, fluffing up her hair.

Trish's coworkers always went out bar-hopping after work on Fridays, and from the sound of their gossip on Monday mornings, they usually met cute guys to hook up with. Now they were pressuring her to join them. She thought about it. It's not like she didn't want to have a special someone in her life someday, but she didn't think she'd meet him at a noisy, crowded bar. She decided to stay true to her personal standards and preferences.

"No thanks, but you all go have fun. It's really not the kind of thing I enjoy," she said.

Working While Autistic

"So what are you going to do, stay home and watch TV alone?" asked Chelsea.

"Or read a book?" added Steph.

"Yes, that sounds like the perfect Friday night for me. See you Monday." Trish waved to them and then shut down her computer and got ready to go. She hoped she hadn't hurt their feelings, but honestly, they'd have a lot more fun without her. Not only did it sound like a sensory and social disaster waiting to happen, but she was also uncomfortable socializing with her colleagues. They worked together, and she wanted to keep their relationship professional. Who knows? Maybe one day she would say yes and see what the bar scene was like, but not today, thank you very much. Friday night with a book and an old science-fiction movie on TV was perfect for Trish.

BILL

Bill read the email from Ned again. "Here's another project you're perfect for! Boss wants it by Friday, so send it to me Thursday. You're the best!"

This was the third project that had come to him through Ned rather than from Mr. Brisbee. He was struggling to finish all of his own work plus these extra projects. Bill needed the knowledge to know what to do about it. He decided to re-read the employee handbook to remind himself what the protocol was for assigning projects to other team members at the same level on the hierarchy.

Bill learned that this shouldn't happen at all. He shouldn't have to do any project Ned sent him, even if he said the boss wanted

Chapter 8

it done. Maybe the boss wanted Ned to do it, and Ned thought it would be easier to hand it off to Bill. Since he always asked for the completed work the day before it was due, chances are he gave it to the boss and pretended he'd done it himself. Bill felt so foolish that he had been taken advantage of, and that he'd let it go on so long.

He decided that, rather than doing Ned's project, he would enlighten their manager. He emailed Mr. Brisbee: "I wanted to inform you that this third project which has been given to me by Ned may take extensive time that I would otherwise devote to the projects you assigned me. Ned tells me that it is a high priority. Is it your recommendation that I prioritize this project above my usual projects? Please advise."

It turned out that Mr. Brisbee had no idea that Ned had been giving his work to Bill to do for him, and he was glad to learn of this. He asked Bill what other projects he had done for Ned, and he was surprised to learn that it had not been Ned's work. Mr. Brisbee told Bill that in the future he was never to accept an assignment from anyone but him, and to notify him if it ever happened again. He also said that he would deal with Ned.

Bill never found out what happened to Ned, which was fine because it was none of his business, but he never got another email from him. By refreshing his knowledge of the hierarchy, reviewing the employee handbook, and enlightening his direct supervisor about the situation, his problem was solved.

Working While Autistic

MARIA

The staff meeting was delayed while the manager took a phone call, so Maria sat silently at the conference table and waited. All around her, conversations ebbed and flowed while she sipped her coffee and did her best to tune them out. Suddenly, one of the voices got louder.

"You're kidding! I can't believe that!"

"It's true, and corporate has no idea! Someone could lose their job over this."

"Who have you told?"

"Who haven't I told! The grapevine always leads back to the boss, so expect fireworks any day now!"

Maria was naturally curious. She wondered if she should ask them what they were talking about, but then she decided against it. This sounded like way too much drama for her liking. She chose to ignore it. Avoiding office gossip was the professional thing to do.

ROBERT

Robert took a deep breath. He hated dealing with the public, but Guy was out of the shop at an appointment. The woman at the counter kept going on and on, demanding a refund. Apparently, the boss had fixed her old radio five years ago, and now it was broken again. She insisted that she should get her entire payment back, since the repair "didn't work." Ridiculous. Old things got older; everyone should know that. Robert kept nodding and taking notes while she droned on. He didn't know what else to do. Is this woman what his daughter called a "Karen"? He'd known plenty of

— Chapter 8 —

women named Karen in his life, and none of them were spoiled, entitled brats. Seemed unfair to sully a perfectly good old-fashioned name like Karen.

Now she said, "I didn't want to play this card, but the customer is always right, so ..." She held out her hand. The woman wanted cash, not credit against another repair, and she expected him to open up the cash drawer and just hand it to her. She didn't even have a receipt to prove she'd ever been there. Robert knew he wasn't up to dealing with her. He had to yield to the boss on this one.

"Ma'am, like I told you, there's no manager here right now, just me. Just write your name and number down here," he pushed a paper and pen toward her, "and I will have the boss call you as soon he gets back. In the meantime, there's nothing I can do for you, so I'll say good-bye and have a nice day." Then he turned his back, put on headphones, and started on the next repair. She kept talking, but he ignored her. He wasn't going to throw her out, but he wasn't going to give her the boss's money, either. This whole thing was above his pay grade, so he yielded to his boss to make the call, and then ignored the rest. It worked for him.

MESSAGES FROM AUTISTIC MENTORS

"With office politics, it's helpful to have a third party to download drama and help figure out next steps."
— Helena, works with autistic children

Working While Autistic

"People where I work wear headsets, and we can hear each other. Sometimes people chat on their headsets between orders. One time coworkers were making fun of someone, so I told my manager. I'm not afraid to be a whistleblower. They were not happy with me, but they were quieter around me after that."

— Suzanne, drive-through window greeter

"Don't listen to gossip; do not step into it. People have to vent sometimes, but when it becomes toxic, just tune it out. I don't want to listen to judgmental talk about other people."

— Beth F. Watzke, late-diagnosed autistic writer and animal care provider

– PART III –
Pivot

"When we are no longer able to change a situation—
we are challenged to change ourselves."
— *Viktor E. Frankl* —

"The only way to make sense out of change is to plunge into it,
move with it, and join the dance."
— *Alan Watts* —

"Don't ever feel trapped in a career path ... Your job should be fun
and rewarding. If it is not, then find something that is."
— *Dr. Temple Grandin and Kate Duffy* —

— CHAPTER 9 —
You're Fired!

"When I was sixteen I worked in a pet store. And they fired me because they had three snakes in there, and one day I braided them."
— *Steven Wright*

"Being fired was the best luck of my life. It made me stop and reflect. It was the birth of my life as a writer."
—*Jose Saramago*

Change, especially unexpected change for the worse, is difficult for anyone to cope with. You may be fired or let go during "downsizing." It's one of those things that can happen to the best of us, but it's hard to accept. Maya Angelou wrote, "If you don't like something, change it. If you can't change it, change your attitude." It is unfortunately true that autistic adults are unemployed and underemployed at a far higher rate than their neuro-majority peers. They also frequently experience unexpected loss of employment. If this happens to you, you probably won't like it and can't change it, so it's smart to try to change your attitude, as Maya Angelou advises, and make a new plan.

Working While Autistic

If you don't have a safety net, such as family who can support you at least temporarily, there is a lot of pressure to get another job immediately so you can maintain the basics of life. Don't make a hasty decision about your next step though. Process what you're going through right now. Remember, most people have been fired or let go at some point in their lives. It doesn't make them a bad person or a failure; it just happens. But when it happens to you, it's traumatic. Take a breath. Take another. You're going to be okay.

If you lose a job you love or that you need, it brings a lot of negative emotions, like anger, embarrassment, depression, shame, or confusion. Positive feelings may also occur, such as relief, freedom, and elation. Usually, there are mixed feelings. I hope you have access to a counselor or mental health practitioner you can talk to, someone who is knowledgeable about neurodiversity. Depression can hit hard and fast, and it's smart to seek professional help to get you through this transitional period. Don't let despair overtake you, or discouragement weigh you down to the point that you are at risk for self-harm. It's not easy to reach out and ask for help, but it is important to do so. Getting fired feels like a big deal. Even though you will have other jobs in the future, right now you are dealing with loss, and this warrants giving yourself the gift of support. Never hesitate to ask for and accept help when you're at a low place in your life. Others have been there and lived to tell the tale. Be encouraged by them and take heart.

Some responses to being fired include the thought, "This is some BS!" You might feel like you've been hit by a truck and need

— Chapter 9 —

to go to the ER. Eventually, in time, you will be ready to TRY again.

Let's use BS, ER, and TRY as acronyms for reacting to and recovering from being unexpectedly fired.

BS

Burnout

The B in BS stands for *burnout*.

Perhaps you got fired because of autistic burnout. It is real, and it affects many autistic people, especially in the workforce. Autistic burnout can overwhelm a person completely. You may find yourself unable to cope with simple tasks that you used to manage with no trouble. You need to remind yourself to eat, drink water, go to the bathroom, sleep, and take care of daily hygiene. It can be too much. If you were fired for tardiness, long lunches, or frequent absences, or if you "spaced out" due to fatigue so that you could not be fully present and productive at work, it may be due to autistic burnout.

It's hard not to take it personally. You try and you try, but it seems like it's never been enough. Devon Price wrote, "The people we've been taught to judge for 'not trying hard enough' are almost invariably the people fighting valiantly against the greatest number of unseen barriers and challenges." Have you felt judged harshly or called lazy? Have you judged yourself for "not trying hard enough"? It's time to give yourself a break. Remind yourself that you are doing the best you can, valiantly, in a neurotypical

Working While Autistic

world that was not built to meet your unique needs. If you burn out running up against unseen barriers, it's not your fault.

I'll say it again: autistic burnout is not your fault. You probably have a different neurology than the other people you work with, but it's not bad or wrong or broken. It's just different. If you try to force yourself into a round hole when you're a perfectly good square peg, it will damage you. The longer you try to mask, ignore your own needs, and avoid asking for support, the harder burnout can hit you. Worse, if you have requested reasonable accommodations and been denied, that's hard to deal with. Maybe losing that job is the best thing for your mental and emotional well-being. Of course, that's a small consolation when you need to make ends meet with no job. Before you put yourself right back on the job market, if you can, take a short breather for yourself first. You don't want to run straight back into another burnout situation.

Self-Care

The S in BS is for *self-care*.

After a traumatic event such as being fired, you need to take some time for self-care. Don't try to "suck it up" and rush into a new job search with no time to heal. Take a break, to the extent that this is possible in your situation. You deserve this time, and future you will thank you when you can avoid repeating a potentially damaging cycle. Self-care looks different for different people. For some it might mean a bubble bath and a good book, or binge-watching a favorite familiar cartoon. For others it might mean a few days in bed with no responsibilities, or a deep dive into your

— Chapter 9 —

favorite interests. Whatever your self-care needs or style, remember to eat food and drink water. Take care of the body you walk around in. You deserve whatever kind of self-care is the most comforting and healing for you.

ER

Evaluate

The E in ER stands for *evaluate*.

Once you have had some time to recover, it's time to take a good, hard look at what happened. If your employer will give you feedback on why they fired you, that's great, but usually they won't because of potential legal ramifications. If you were written up or put on an improvement plan before you lost your job, review the paperwork. What can you learn from the path that led to your termination? Be honest with yourself about areas or behaviors that your employer saw as negative. Rather than being defensive, review it with an eye to see what you can learn from this experience. Being in denial will not help you, because the same issues may come up with any new job you pursue. Find out what didn't work for your employer, and see if these are things you can change, and want to change. Ask yourself if these are areas where accommodations would have helped you stay in that job. If you evaluate what went wrong before you lost this job, it will help you in your next one.

Working While Autistic

Regroup

The R in ER stands for *regroup*.

Once you have evaluated what went wrong in your previous job, it's time to regroup before you get back out on your job search. Think about your field of employment. Is it a good fit for your strengths and needs? Is there a different career you could pivot to rather than another job in the same industry? These are important questions to ask yourself after your termination. Ask people who know you well and whose opinions you trust for their input as you regroup and prepare to get back on the job market.

TRY

Temp Work

The T in TRY stands for *temp work*.

While you wait for your ideal next job, consider temporary work to fill in and help pay the bills in the interim. This is not for everyone, but it might be a good "now" solution for you and give you time to plan carefully what your next career move should be.

If you are someone who does great in job interviews but struggles to maintain that high level over time, temporary work may be right for you. If you have a need for variety in your life and crave novelty, you should try temp work. Even if you hate a job, if it's only for a short time, you might find you can put up with it and get your paycheck before you have a chance to burn out. With temp work, you can experiment with different types of

— Chapter 9 —

work. You can also get to know various companies. If you get an assignment where there's an obnoxious workplace bully, you don't have to live with it. If you get an assignment you love, let them know you're interested in long-term employment and ask if they have any openings. This is a chance for you to test the waters to see how you like working there, and it lets them see your strengths.

On the other hand, if you're a person who hates change and takes a long time to adjust to anything new, this is probably not the best fit for you. Think about what it would take for you to be able to tolerate different workplaces for short periods of time. If this is your idea of a nightmare, then do not do this.

Restricted Hours

The R in TRY stands for *restricted hours*.

You may be someone who can tolerate your job for a limited amount of time, but not eight hours a day, five days a week. If so, look for part-time work. It's better to get a smaller paycheck and have time to recover from the social and sensory stressors at work than to try to work full-time and burn out again. Honor your needs. This is not "lazy." Someone who stresses and worries about work and tries so hard that they burn out is definitely not a lazy person. Devon Price wrote, "The Laziness Lie is a deep-seated, culturally held belief system that leads many of us to believe the following: Deep down I'm lazy and worthless. I must work incredibly hard, all the time, to overcome my inner laziness. My worth is earned through my productivity. Work is the center of life. Anyone who isn't accomplished and driven is immoral. The Laziness Lie is the source of the guilty feeling that we are not 'doing enough'; it's also the force that compels us to work ourselves to sickness." Don't believe the lie. Be kind to yourself. Be honest with your next employer about how many hours per week you can maintain while you also prioritize self-care to support your mental and emotional well-being. You are worthy of self-care.

Yes to You

The Y in TRY stands for saying *yes to you*.

You deserve to prioritize your personal health and happiness over your employer's bottom line. They may try to pressure you to work overtime, extend your available hours, or work in the office when working from home is most productive for you. You may want to consult with an advocate to protect yourself from undue pressure. Each time you say, "No," to your employer, you say, "Yes," to yourself. You deserve it.

SIX CHARACTERS IN SEARCH OF EMPLOYMENT

DAISY

DAISY: You're firing me?

LILAC: I'm not firing you. It's just the end of your Work Study, so this will be your last week.

DAISY: But I don't want to stop working here! I love it!

— Chapter 9 —

LILAC: You have your whole life ahead of you, and you will find the career that is right for you. I've enjoyed getting to know you, but you always knew this would be a temporary assignment.

DAISY: I naturally assumed that you would see what a good worker I am and offer me a job at the end of the semester. Not that you'd fire me!

LILAC: Again, you are not being fired, but this is the end of your job here.

DAISY: Why can't I keep working for you as a regular employee after the Work Study?

LILAC: It's just not an option, Daisy. And there's another thing.

NARRATOR: *What other blow can she bestow on poor, wounded Peridot Goldhammer the Mighty, now fallen?*

LILAC: I wanted to tell you about the evaluation form I filled out for your teacher.

DAISY: Evaluation form? Are you grading me?

LILAC: Mr. Worth grades all the students in the course, but with input from your onsite supervisor, which is me.

DAISY: So, how did I do?

Working While Autistic

LILAC: I marked you as "Exceeds expectations" for Attendance and Punctuality. I'm not counting that first day; you were never late again, and I appreciate that. You also exceeded expectations for Quality of Work and met expectations for Initiative and Flexibility.

DAISY: Great, that must be everything important, right?

LILAC: There's more. I had to mark you as "Does not meet expectations" for Judgment & Decision-Making, Communication, and Teamwork & Cooperation.

NARRATOR: *Our hero felt as if she had received a death blow, but from a supposed comrade in arms rather than a known enemy. She could not speak.*

LILAC: There have been times when you needed explicit instructions repeated multiple times and you seemed unable to make decisions independently, particularly when it came to customer interactions. Sometimes you talk to yourself aloud in quite a different voice, and people have been put off by it.

NARRATOR: *Egads! She heard us?*

— Chapter 9 —

LILAC: Also, you never seemed to put any effort into getting along with your classmate, Caitlin, and there were conflicts between you. I know these are areas affected by autism, and I'm sure Mr. Worth will not reduce your classroom grade because of it, but I owe it to you to be honest about your first work experience. These are things that I firmly believe you can work on and improve, and maturity will help. You have a bright future ahead of you, Daisy, I am sure of it. I will miss you, but I wish you all the best in your next work experience. You are probably the most unique and interesting student I have ever had here, and I'm glad we met.

NARRATOR: *Nothing could pierce the dark clouds that followed our hero as she left Lilacs & Lattes for the final time. She fell into a deep depression and took to her bed for two long, lonely days. Finally, the matriarch convinced her to eat by preparing her favorite foods. Although she was sure she couldn't eat a bite, once she smelled the macaroni and cheese and saw the crisp, ultra-browned breadcrumb topping, she realized she was as ravenous as The Hungry, a demon she encountered once in a D&D game. After she had eaten her fill, she turned to her phone to bring forth videos of D&D games, and*

Working While Autistic

NARRATOR: *soon lost herself binge-watching the familiar adventures she loved. Eventually, she emerged sufficiently to bathe, and she began to feel human again, or at least, as close to human as a chaotic good dwarf could feel. By treating herself with loving care and patience as she recovered from the unexpected ending of the job she loved, she was able to heal and once more face the world with courage and determination to learn from this experience.*
(continued)

ZACH

"I hate to let you go," said Martin, on-site supervisor of the assisted-living facility where Zach worked, "but since you were promoted to full-time, your employment here has been kind of all over the place. Sometimes you are the most responsible and productive person on the team. Other times you are forgetful, withdrawn, and slow to respond. And to be honest, you don't look happy to be here."

"But I am happy to be here," Zach said. "I love this job! I'm just not good at making the right facial expressions."

"Don't make up excuses. Everybody makes facial expressions, it's natural, and your face looks like you don't want to be here at all."

"I really don't know how to do facial expressions like the rest of you do. I'm autistic. Maybe I should have told you before."

"I had no idea," said Martin. "Okay, so you're telling me you're happy even when your face looks blank or sad or angry?"

— Chapter 9 —

"Right. I've never felt sad or angry here. That's just my face." Zach looked down at his hands on his knees. "I guess I'd better work on the facial expression thing."

"That's not the main reason we're letting you go, Zach. It's your inconsistency. You're either our hardest worker or a complete slacker. I never know if you're going to be asking for more work or hiding. You don't seem like a lazy person, but sometimes I have to say you do act like one. Is that related to autism?"

"I'm not lazy! I want to work, but I get autistic burnout. After a few hours it can hit me, and I feel completely drained, like I don't want to see another person or do another thing for the rest of the day. I'm sorry, but I can't seem to do anything about it."

"What about working fewer hours? You always do so well in the mornings, but in the afternoons you're like another person."

"Afternoons are hard for me."

"I have an idea. The new part-time guy we just hired would love to be full-time. Would you be willing to reduce your hours to mornings, and I can increase his hours?"

"Actually, that would be great! I definitely want to keep working here, but if I keep pushing myself to work through burnout, I'm afraid it could affect my health."

"I had no idea, but I'm glad we won't have to lose you, Zach. I'll make the arrangements, and I'll let you know when your hours will be cut back. And let me know if there's anything else I can do for you."

For Zach, the perfect solution to his afternoon burn-out was to reduce his working hours. Financially, he would take a hit, but

Working While Autistic

since he lived at the temple where he was a caretaker, he'd be okay as long as he watched his spending. It was a huge relief not to be fired after all.

TRISH

Throughout Trish's career working for the college she had attended, there had been times that she needed to evaluate her career goals.

When the global pandemic shut down her college temporarily, she got a pink slip, a termination notice. She was fired! It was devastating, even though she realized everyone in her department had received one. They put a halt to all admissions activities while they shifted to online courses so that the current students' educations would not be interrupted. They couldn't accept any new students during the chaos of restructuring, so they couldn't pay for the admissions department staff. Trish found herself at home with nothing to do, and she struggled to cope. Sometimes she went to the campus and walked around the empty grounds; the exercise seemed to do her good. She spent her days reading. Fortunately, she could get lost in a book series and forget about her own troubles for a while.

Eventually, the college regrouped and started to re-hire the admissions staff to work from home. Trish was thrilled to get the word that she would have her old job back. She was especially delighted to work from home. She loved being in her own familiar space. Having productive work to do and having an income again before she ran through unemployment and her savings was a huge relief!

– Chapter 9 –

In time, the college built itself back up, students returned to campus, and the future looked hopeful again. As much as she had loved working from home, when she was told to return to the office, it never occurred to Trish to question the requirement. She had always been a firm follower of rules, and she did as she was told, even though she had felt so much more comfortable and productive from home. She didn't even evaluate what it would mean for her. She simply responded to what was important for the college.

BILL

Every once in a while, when he was particularly anxious or stressed, Bill's mind took him on a tour of everything he had ever done wrong in his life. Each awkward conversation when he thought of the snappy comeback hours later would replay, and he would re-live the embarrassment. Every time he had been turned down for a date, or not invited to a party, or bullied, it all came back in a doom spiral that he had trouble shaking. This was one of those days.

One of his brain's favorite failure stories to replay was the time he got fired. Bill was eighteen years old, and it was his first job as a college freshman. He worked in the campus dining hall kitchen. It was hot, smelly, and noisy, and Bill could hardly breathe, much less work. He took long breaks and hid in the bathroom. Some days he could not bring himself to get out of bed and drag himself to work. He was depressed, and it affected his grades too. It was almost a relief when the manager told him he was fired. Almost.

Working While Autistic

The main feeling he had was that of failure and self-loathing. If he couldn't even do a mindless job like this, how would he ever make it as an adult? He wished he could just sleep and forget about college. Fortunately, his advisor talked him out of dropping out. When he heard about Bill's experience in the dining hall, he pulled some strings and got him a job in the library. It was quiet, and it smelled like books. Heaven! The only downside was that they let students come in and check out books. Oh well, there was no getting around that.

Usually when Bill started to spiral into a depression, his memory of that time of his life stopped at the point where he got fired. This time, though, he pushed forward through the bad memory to what came next, his library job, and how his life had improved since then. Getting fired from that dining hall job was actually a good thing. It meant he could find something that suited him better. The library job was a start, and he went on to a career he loved in IT.

For Bill, moving on from a past failure was saying yes to himself. He decided to get up and go for a walk to help shake off his dark mood. There was a lovely college campus nearby. He'd walk through it, enjoying the towering trees and the classic architecture of the old buildings. He figured the exercise would do him good, and he was right.

— Chapter 9 —

MARIA

"It's not that you haven't done a good job, Maria. We want you to know that. It's just that, as a small company, we must cut corners where we can in order to remain viable."

"So you're cutting ... my corner?" Maria wasn't sure what they meant by that.

"Yes, sadly, we're going to have to let you go."

"You don't want me to keep proofreading books for you?"

"We found that artificial intelligence can proofread much faster, and, well, we don't have to put AI on the payroll."

"So there's a free way to do my job? Like with a robot?" Maria was intrigued.

"Not a robot, but we can access a pro AI manuscript analysis program for a couple of hundred dollars a year. Total! We couldn't say no to that. Which, unfortunately, means that we have to say goodbye to you."

"Oh." Maria didn't know what she was supposed to say.

"We'll give you an excellent recommendation, of course."

"Of course. I mean, thank you. So ... what do I do now?"

"Since you don't have a desk here to clear out, you don't have to do anything. Your final paycheck will be deposited in your account."

"I see," said Maria.

She didn't quite see, but what else was there to say? Her supervisor and the HR department manager stood up, so she stood up too. They glanced at the door, so she did too.

"So I'll be leaving now?" It came out like a question.

Working While Autistic

"Yes, yes, all the best to you going forward, Maria. It's been a pleasure having you on the team. Goodbye now." The HR manager opened the door for her, and she walked out, a bit shaky.

It took several hours for Maria to fully process that she had been fired. They had found a cheaper online program to do her job, and she was out. Were computers really taking over the world? If they did, she wanted a giant robot of her own to ride around in. But she knew that was not reality. Getting fired was reality.

What would she do now?

For a week she stayed home, which was normal, and spent a lot of time watching sloths on the internet. She also binge-watched all of her favorite movies and cartoons about giant transforming robots. These things helped her feel more balanced, grounded. She longed to feel as calm as a sloth and as brave as a giant robot, but she still felt sad and shaky.

Eventually she decided to do something before her final paycheck was gone with no new checks arriving. She searched online for proofreading jobs. What she found was a temporary agency that hired people for short-term positions. This seemed manageable somehow. If she could still work from home and avoid in-person meetings, temporary work might suit her to a T.

After reading her letter of recommendation, which was glowing as promised, the temp agency recommended her to small publishers and independent authors who paid by the piece, not an hourly wage or salary.

Maria loved the temporary work. They would send her a single manuscript to proof, and she would do it in her own time,

— **Chapter 9** —

and when she returned it to the publisher, they paid her. The more she accepted, the more she got paid. Since she could focus and work efficiently, she soon found that she could bring in about as much money as she had in her previous job. Temporary work, being paid by work product rather than by the hour, was right for Maria.

ROBERT

"Got another old TV for you." Guy pointed to the 1960s-era set, maple wood with angled legs made to stand on the floor rather than sit on a desk or hang on the wall. "They want the wooden console refinished. I know it's not your usual job, but do you know how to do it?"

"Sure thing, I've refinished plenty of old maple furniture. Dressers, a crib, I can refinish that and make it look like new."

"Great. They don't want the insides, mind you, just the console. We're going to fix up a modern flat screen inside of it. I guess they want it to look old but work like new."

Robert shook his head. "What will they think of next? But, sure, I can do that. Sand it down, match the color of the maple varnish and everything."

"Thanks, I figured you'd be up for it." Guy turned back to the laptop he was repairing.

Robert ran his hands across the wooden surface and peered into the back at the good old cathode-ray tube inside. Back in the day, before retirement, he would have gotten this set working like new. It only needed a few parts and some adjustments. But nobody

Working While Autistic

wanted old TVs fixed anymore, not when they could buy a giant flat-screen LCD set.

Robert thought back to his last day of working for his old company, before he was pushed into retirement. No, call it what it was: he was fired. They said he was too old to make the transition to the new technology and there was no place for him anymore. That sure hit him hard—made him feel like a swaybacked, long-in-the-tooth old horse, put out to pasture. At least they didn't shoot him or send him to the glue factory. How had he even survived that horrible time after he lost the job he loved so much for so long? Oh yeah, he remembered, it was Helen. She just kept loving him right through the rough patch, loved him enough to let him wallow in it for a while, and then gave him a kick in the pants when she figured that's what he needed. Helen always knew. He had to pivot, regroup, and figure out what was next. Of course they could live on social security and what they'd put away for retirement, but what kind of life was that, sitting around doing nothing, feeling sorry for himself?

One of the best things that had happened to him, besides Helen, Lena, and Bobby, and after the Old Geezers' Club at the diner, was this part-time job with Guy. He felt useful again. He figured that even when something terrible happened, like getting fired, there was always a way forward. And going forward, you were sure to find new opportunities and experiences. Robert hoped he'd never be too old to try something new.

— Chapter 9 —

MESSAGES FROM AUTISTIC MENTORS

"I've been fired twice because people didn't like me. One of them thought that I would not be a whistleblower, but I was. In another job, they didn't think I would speak up for the rights of the children, but I did, so they found an excuse to get rid of me. I never got written up, just terminated immediately. If this happens to you, file for unemployment and take an emotional six-month break if you can. It takes time to regroup and re-energize. Get therapy or coaching, and give yourself grace to forgive yourself for getting fired. If you can afford to live on unemployment, take time to re-empower yourself before you get back to work."

— Suzanne, drive-through window greeter

"Two of the hardest things for me have been working for fools and holding my tongue when I saw injustice. If my boss had a stupid idea, it would be difficult for me to filter how I responded to it. I had a tendency to be brutally honest, which never ended well. If I saw that a coworker was being bullied, I would just blurt out what a jerk the boss was and tell them they couldn't treat people that way. I lost a couple of jobs because I didn't control those impulses. As I matured and understood more about myself, especially knowing now that I'm autistic, I learned to stop and think before I jump right in. I have to ask myself, is action required? Maybe holding my tongue for now and bringing it up later will let me do the right thing and still keep my job. The older I get, the more important

Working While Autistic

this is. I may need a job, but I also know I can't ignore injustice. Taking the time to figure out the best way to address a problem and asking for advice from someone I trust is important for me."

— Scott

"It wasn't presented to me as they were firing me, but they said it wasn't working out and they were letting me go. I said, 'Okay, I'm sorry it didn't work out.' I asked for a reference, and they gave me one. Once I worked for a two-partner business, and one partner just said, you can go. It felt mean. Know your rights. I still have to learn my rights as an autist. Accept it, and ask for a reference and feedback if you want to. If you're emotional, that's okay. Tell yourself that you took a blow with grace and now you can take care of yourself. Meditate, rest, use positive self-talk, give yourself a hug, call a friend, hug your pet, go for a walk, and stay hydrated. If you have a community who understands, reach out. Take care of yourself."

— Beth F. Watzke, late-diagnosed autistic writer and animal care provider

– CHAPTER 10 –
I Quit!

"If at first you don't succeed, try, try again. Then quit. There's no point in being a damn fool about it."

— *W. C. Fields*

"All ballplayers should quit when it starts to feel as if all the baselines run uphill."

— *Babe Ruth*

You may have a job now, but that doesn't mean you're stuck with it forever if it's not right for you. You might think, "I'm no quitter!" And that's true. Quitters are slackers, deserters, people who never follow through on anything. That's not you. You may have a critical voice in your head right now calling you all those names, but that voice lies to you. It lies! When you've tried and tried, when you've pushed yourself through the maze of social and sensory overload to stay with a job as long as you can until you burn out, you are not a quitter. You are a survivor. Good for you! Tell that critical voice in your head, "Scoot! Be off with you! And don't darken my brain again!"

Working While Autistic

There are many issues that might point toward quitting as your best option. Let's use the word ISSUES to discuss them: *interpersonal issues*, *sensory issues*, *social issues*, *uncertainty issues*, *expectation issues*, and *sanity issues*.

ISSUES

Interpersonal Issues

The I in ISSUES stands for *interpersonal issues*.

If you have a bully in your workplace, it can make it impossible to stay without sacrificing your mental health. Sometimes your bully may be a colleague, or even your manager or HR. If someone messes with you and then gaslights you to make you think it's your fault, that's a difficult place to work. Far too many autistic people have a traumatic history of being the target of bullying since childhood, not just from classmates but from teachers and others in authority. It can make it hard to distinguish between what's "normal" behavior and what's bullying. If you're not sure if it's actual bullying or typical banter, look around to see if they treat everyone the way they treat you. If they do, it doesn't necessarily mean they're not a bully, just that you're not their only target. Choose someone you trust, such as a spouse, family member, friend, or counselor, someone who does not work with you, to consult with. Tell them about the incidents and see if they perceive them as bullying or if they think it's normal workplace behavior. Still, even if they say it's normal, if you can't tolerate it, you don't have

Chapter 10

to stay in that job. Talk to HR about this if there's a hostile work environment, unless HR is the bully. Ask about reassignment to a different area to escape the bully. Working from home would go a long way toward solving this issue. If all else fails, it may be time to look for another job. You have a right to feel safe at work.

Sensory Issues

The first S in ISSUES stands for *sensory issues*.

You may have an extremely sensitive sense of smell or hearing, or other heightened senses. If you work in an open office, you might smell everyone's perfume or tuna fish or hear the squeak of every chair, the taps on every keyboard, and every word of every telephone conversation. It may be nearly impossible for you to focus on your own work. Try strategies to protect yourself, such as a face mask with a drop of vanilla or another scent that you enjoy, or noise-canceling headphones. If these don't work and you have asked for and been denied accommodations that would help, such as working from home, it may be time for you to move on. You deserve a sensory-safe environment.

Social Issues

The second S in ISSUES stands for *social issues*.

You may work in an office with an "open door" culture where colleagues drop in on one another to consult on work-related topics, or to chat. If you are uncomfortable with drop-in social butterflies but feel pressured to keep your office door open, this may not be the right environment for you. If you have disclosed

Working While Autistic

your autism at work, they should approve your request to keep your door closed, to attend only meetings that are relevant to you, or to work from home. If none of these things are approved for you, and you need privacy to be productive, it may be time for you to look for employment elsewhere.

Uncertainty Issues

The U in ISSUES stands for *uncertainty issues*.

Perhaps you are one of the many people who thrive on clear expectations. You like to know exactly what you are supposed to do, when it should be completed, and who to turn it in to when you're done. You might find yourself working for a company that is not well-organized. If the hierarchy seems to shift so that you're never quite sure who your direct supervisor is, or if your job description is vague and changes depending on who you talk to, this could be incredibly stressful for you. Some people thrive in this kind of wishy-washy environment, but others do not. Ask for expectations to be specified clearly in writing, with due dates and hierarchy of supervision; these are reasonable accommodations. If the company is unwilling or unable to provide certainty and clarity, that could be your cue to put yourself back on the job market.

Expectation Issues

The E in ISSUES stands for *expectation issues*.

There may be an imbalance in what is expected of you in your job. If your contract states that you will work from 9:00 AM until 5:00 PM with a half-hour lunch, then you should be able to leave

— Chapter 10 —

the office for your lunch break and go home at 5:00 PM. Your free time is your own, time to do anything or nothing at all, and it's worth protecting. Devon Price writes in *Laziness Does Not Exist*, "'Wasting time' is a basic human need. Once we accept that, we can stop fearing our inner 'laziness' and begin to build healthy, happy, well-balanced lives." You are not lazy. However, some employers may have a hidden agenda. They may expect that someone who is a "team player" and wants to advance will come in early, work through lunch, stay late, and answer emails and phone calls after hours. This is an unreasonable expectation. Unless they pay you overtime to stay late, you have every right to work the hours you are paid to work, and no more. If someone emails you on the weekend, you may respond first thing Monday morning. If you feel harassed to meet their unrealistic expectations, you have a right to stand up for yourself. If the expectations are intolerable, look for another job. This is important. I know I've said it before, but I want you to hear it: You are not lazy. You are doing the job you were hired for, working the hours you are paid for, and the rest of your time is your own. You deserve it.

Sanity Issues

The last S in ISSUES stands for *sanity issues*.

Are they driving you crazy at work? Are you at risk of burnout? Is your mental or physical health suffering because of this job? Your sanity and mental health are important. Prioritize yourself over your job; it's the smart thing to do. You deserve self-care. If you quit a job to honor your own needs, it doesn't make you a "quitter,"

Working While Autistic

it makes you a responsible person who knows your strengths, your needs, and your limits. Honor yourself. It's the right thing to do.

You may have reviewed all of the ISSUES that make it difficult for you to remain in your current position, and you realize now that you need to leave. How should you go about it? Use QUIT for suggestions: *quiet quitting*; *union rep*; *exit interview*; and *tell, thank, take a walk*.

QUIT

Quiet Quitting

The Q in QUIT stands for *quiet quitting*.

This is a misnomer, as it does not involve actually quitting. Many people decide that they will no longer give in to pressure to work beyond the hours they are paid for. They come into the office on time, take their full lunch break, and leave on the dot at the end of their shift. They do not respond to messages that come in outside of their working hours until they get back to work the next day. Obviously, this isn't quitting at all since they are still doing the job they were hired for to earn their paycheck. The fact that this practice has been called *quiet quitting* highlights the problem of employers who expect more out of their employees than they pay for. If you can remain in your current job and refuse to go above and beyond the basic requirements, that's great! You can continue to get paid without having to go back on the job market. If you are fired for doing your job and no more, you may have cause to

– Chapter 10 –

challenge it, or you may be relieved and collect unemployment while you look for a better job.

Union

The U in QUIT stands for *union*.

If you are in a union, meet with your union representative and tell them about your issues with the company. They are on your side. Ask them about the best way to inform the company that you quit, and ask them to come with you when you tell HR. You might think that HR would advocate for you, since you are one of the humans in Human Resources, but HR works for the company, not the workers. They will prioritize your boss's interests and will not go to bat for you against the company. Your union rep represents you. If you don't have a union and you want to meet with HR to tell them you are leaving, bring an advocate or support person with you. It's good to have someone on your side when you deliver bad news, especially if it's hard for you to express yourself when under stress.

Interview

The I in QUIT stands for *exit interview*.

Many companies want to hold an exit interview before you leave. They might use this interview for one of three reasons. Reason one: they want to try to convince you to stay. If they can offer enough to make you change your mind, such as a pay increase, promotion, and accommodations you need, then it's a win-win. They've won you over, so you don't have to quit. However, there might be a

Working While Autistic

couple of other reasons. Reason two: they want to find out why you're leaving because they really want to improve how they do business, in order to avoid losing other valuable workers. Reason three: they are required to fill in a form and they have to go through the motions. You may choose to attend the exit interview, or you may be able to opt out of it or provide your reasons for leaving by email rather than in person. Unless you signed a contract agreeing to an exit interview before you quit, you're not obligated to attend.

Tell Them, Thank Them, Take a Walk

The T in QUIT stands for three things: *tell them, thank them, take a walk.*

Obviously, you need to *tell them* you are leaving their employ, and by what date. If you have paid vacation days coming, be sure to take those days before you leave. Next, *thank them* for the opportunity or experience. They may not deserve thanks if you have been treated poorly, but it is an act of grace and a sign of maturity to give thanks regardless. It costs you nothing. If you want a recommendation from them, you will want to leave on a good note rather than dumping all your frustrations on them. Finally, *take a walk*. Go. Just go. Don't look back. You're off on your next adventure, and it's smart and healthy to leave the past behind. Don't rewind and replay it. Just let it go. You are free!

Let's check in with our six characters and see how they dealt with quitting issues.

— Chapter 10 —

SIX CHARACTERS IN SEARCH OF EMPLOYMENT

DAISY

Daisy's second Work Study assignment was at a pet store. Because she enjoyed nature and animals, Mr. Worth thought it would be a good fit for her. She loved socializing the kittens and puppies to prepare them for their new forever homes, and she was good at stocking and organizing the shelves. Everything was going fine, until ...

BOSS: Daisy? I've got a new assignment for you.

DAISY: Sure, anything you say, Boss.

BOSS: You don't have to call me boss, you know.

DAISY: I like calling you boss, Boss.

NARRATOR: *What was the man's name? Our hero was nervous on her first day and did not process it, but now it was too late to ask. Curse the lack of name badges at this job!*

BOSS: Okaaay. Anyway, let me show you the pinkies.

NARRATOR: *Pinkies? What was the boss talking about, little fingers? This made no sense. More information is needed.*

DAISY: Pinkies?

Working While Autistic

BOSS: Yeah, the baby mice.

DAISY: Baby mice? Oh, yeah, pinkies! Like Pinky and the Brain!

BOSS: ... Anywaay, this is where we keep them.

DAISY: How cute! Do they need socializing before they're adopted?

BOSS: No, these are not fancy mice sold as pets. They're white feeder mice.

DAISY: Feeder mice? Do you need me to feed them?

BOSS: Yes, you can feed them to Monty, our python.

NARRATOR: *Daisy is appalled. She cannot have heard correctly.*

DAISY: ... You want me to ... feed ... the mice ... to ...

BOSS: Yes, to Monty. Today is his feeding day. It's easy, just like this. *(He tosses a pinky into the enclosure, and Monty begins to uncoil.)*

DAISY: NONONONONONONO!

BOSS: Hey, calm down! You're scaring Monty!

DAISY: Animal cruelty! Animal cruelty! Call 911!

BOSS: Whoa, nobody is calling 911. Get ahold of yourself! This is part of the job.

– Chapter 10 –

DAISY: I quit! I will not be a party to this tragedy! I'm leaving, and I will report you, you- you-

NARRATOR: *Our hero proceeded to call her ex-boss every monstrous name in the official Dungeons & Dragons Monster Handbook as she ran out of the store. She finally stopped running after a block, caught her breath, and called her mother to pick her up. Never again would she darken the door of this horrendous establishment. Never again!*

Mr. Worth listened to her side of the story and agreed that this would not be an appropriate Workability site for Daisy after all, especially after the way she quit. Fortunately, Lilac was happy to let Daisy return to Lilacs & Lattes for another semester, so catastrophe was averted. The pet store had seemed like a good idea, but it was not a good fit for Daisy. Although she realized later that there are probably fifty ways to leave your employer that do not involve name-calling, at the time, she saw no alternative. She had no real regrets.

ZACH

Zach stood outside the rabbi's door with his hand up, about to knock. He thought back to seven years ago when he had first knocked on this door to ask about the caretaker job. It had been a *b'racha*, a blessing, to have been hired and given an apartment here at the temple. It allowed him to move out of his parents' home

Working While Autistic

and to finally feel like a productive member of the community. He owed so much, and he was grateful. This was a conversation he dreaded but couldn't avoid. He knocked.

"Come in, Zachary. Right on time, I see."

"Thank you for seeing me, Rabbi."

"I always have time for you, my boy. Tell me, what is so serious that you should come here with such a look? What is wrong?"

"Nothing is wrong, Rabbi. Actually, everything is wonderful. You know I've been seeing Crystal?"

"A lovely young woman. Your mother has told me of her sterling qualities, many times."

"Well, I've asked her to marry me, and she said yes."

"Mazel tov! Congratulations! I am so happy for you both!" The rabbi stood and shook Zach's hand enthusiastically. "You should be smiling! What can be troubling you, with news this wonderful?"

"Well, you know how grateful I am for the position of caretaker and for the apartment," Zach began, unsure how to go on.

"And now it is time for you to move on. Is that what you don't want to tell me?"

"Yes!" Zach breathed a sigh and felt his shoulders relax. "I'm not ungrateful, but over the years I've been given a promotion at my other job, and together, Crystal and I can afford an apartment of our own."

"Of course! This is the natural state of affairs. We knew you would not be our live-in caretaker forever."

"You knew?"

— Chapter 10 —

"Of course! You are a bright young man, and you have a good future ahead of you. Your work with us was a steppingstone, not a millstone around your neck."

"I'm so relieved, Rabbi! Here is my letter of resignation."

"I accept it with my congratulations and all good wishes for you and your future, Zach. Again, mazel tov!"

Zach had dreaded this meeting, and it was a huge weight off his shoulders that his rabbi was not disappointed in him. He was grateful for this start, but now he was ready to begin his new life with Crystal.

TRISH

Trish looked down into Baby James's face as he slept in her arms. She was filled with an intensity of love she wouldn't have thought possible. She thought back over the last few wonderful years.

When Trish met and fell in love with Bill and they began their life together, for the first time in her working life, there was something more important to her than her job. When they added Baby James to their family, she had to evaluate her priorities.

She saw a drop of water fall on the blanket and realized she was crying. How could she leave her baby to go back to work? She could not imagine how it would feel to walk out that door and not see this sweet face again for hours. There were so many things to do. She would have to pump at work to provide milk for the baby. They would have to find reliable childcare they could trust. Bill worked from home, but he couldn't work and care for Baby James. Trish knew that most of the women she worked with had children at home, and many had returned after six weeks of maternity leave. It couldn't have been easy for them, but women were strong. Mothers could do difficult things. But was she strong enough? She didn't know.

When she told Bill how she felt, he said she should quit. He would provide for the family, and she shouldn't have to work if she wanted to stay home with Baby James. But was that what she wanted, really? She loved her job, too, but not as much as she loved being a mommy.

With Bill's encouragement, she wrote a letter of resignation and emailed it to her supervisor two weeks before her paid maternity leave was up. The college made a counter-offer. They would grant her six more weeks of maternity leave and hold her job for her. At the end of that leave, they offered to allow her to work from home, part-time if that's what she needed, and to only come to campus for required staff meetings. Trish and Bill were thrilled, and she accepted the offer immediately. She wouldn't have to lose the job she loved simply because she loved her family more.

BILL

Bill hated office gossip, and it was easy to ignore it when working from home. One day, though, when he came in for the monthly mandatory in-person meeting, the chatter was deafening. Word was that their small computer startup was so successful the owner was selling it to a big conglomerate for "beaucoup bucks," as Ned told everyone. People worried about layoffs, especially departments that would be duplicated, like HR. It's not like the new corporation

— Chapter 10 —

would need two HR departments, so they were already sending out resumés. The tension in the air made it hard for Bill to breathe. He felt buried in tribbles, like in the fifteenth episode of the second season of the original *Star Trek*, "The Trouble with Tribbles." He replayed the episode in his head, and it helped him relax temporarily. Before long, though, the tension was back, and he couldn't draw a comfortable breath until he got out of the meeting and back home again.

Later he learned that he would have two choices: he could continue to work for the new corporation after the takeover, but he would have to be 100 percent back in the office. Or he could quit and find another job where he could work from home. Mr. Brisbee promised him a sterling letter of recommendation, and even knew someone who was looking for an employee like Bill. It might mean a pay cut though.

Bill thought about his choices long and hard. Finally, he realized that he could not be happy or productive working in-office for a huge corporation. He would rather quit and get back into the job search to find a place where he could work from home. With Mr. Brisbee's help, he did find a job where he felt he could be happy. Their office was in a nice neighborhood, across the street from the local college where he liked to walk. When he had to go in for the occasional in-person meeting, he could reward himself afterward with a stroll through the quiet campus with its large trees and the sound of the fountain outside the admissions building. For Bill, leaving on his own before the layoffs began was smart, as he could avoid being fired and find a position that suited him and met his needs. Quitting a corporate job that promised more money, but also more stress, was a no-brainer for Bill.

MARIA

Maria loved the temp work that was sent to her from small, independent publishing companies. She knew she was good at it, and they always accepted her edits with no arguments. The authors, on the other hand, were a different story. They wanted to be personally involved and question every edit. Why hire her if they didn't want to let her do her job?

One writer was particularly annoying. She had written a five hundred thousand-word fantasy-speculative fiction book, planned to be the first in an eight-part series. She wanted Maria to "touch it up" so she could send it to a publisher and get a big advance. Maria thought the chances of that were miniscule, but it was not her job to provide a reality check.

Unfortunately, this writer questioned every correction that Maria made, and often demanded that she change it back. The woman would not accept a single space after a period because she had gotten an A in typing in high school, back in the day, so she knew what was proper. No amount of explanation could convince her that a double space after a period was no longer correct. She also used quotation marks, italics, and boldface intermittently to emphasize words she said were important. She even balked when Maria corrected her erratically shifting verb tenses because, as she said, "I wrote it that way because of the way the words flowed. Poetic license must be respected."

— Chapter 10 —

Finally, the day that the writer sent Maria a six hundred-word email discussing the pros and cons of the Oxford comma and asked Maria to respond to each of the twenty-seven points, Maria had had enough. Life was too short to put up with this persnickety person, who would never be the next Ursula Le Guin or Anne McCaffrey, whatever she might think. She wanted to quit. But how should she go about it?

Maria struggled to put her thoughts about working with this writer into words without insulting her. Then she realized that she didn't have to tell the writer she quit; she just had to tell the temp agency. They would tell the writer. What a relief!

As it turned out, Maria was the fourth proofreader who had tried to work with this writer, and each of the others had quit far sooner than she had. Her contact at the agency said not to worry about it, they'd take care of it, and they probably wouldn't even assign another temp to the writer since she'd been so difficult to work with. Maria was flooded with relief as she realized that never again would she have to read an email from that demanding writer. Quitting was the best option for her.

ROBERT

Robert's first job was as an audio-visual (AV) assistant at a high school. He was barely out of school himself, so he felt pretty comfortable in the setting, and he loved tinkering with the AV equipment and getting things working again when they were out of kilter. Most of the time, though, he pushed a big, wheeled stand with a TV or projector on it from class to class, when teachers

Working While Autistic

needed to show a film or access the Spanish language lessons on television. He would get a note from the AV manager with the equipment needed, room number, and what time it was needed, and he'd push it over there and then bring it back to the AV storage when they were done with it.

That first year, there was a senior who used to taunt him about his lowly job. Robert was only a year older than the boy, and the bullying stung him. He put up with it silently for a while. He figured if he ignored the teasing, it would stop. That didn't happen though. When the boy couldn't get a rise out of him by jeering, laughing, and name-calling, he took his bullying to the next level.

He'd put his foot out as Robert wheeled the AV cart by, acting as if he were going to kick it over. Then when Robert flinched and grabbed the handles harder, he laughed, along with the rest of his crowd. When Robert got used to the fake kicks and didn't react, the boy went further still, until finally he did tip the cart over. The TV was held to the cart by strong canvas straps so it couldn't fly across the hallway and hit anyone, but it did shatter when it hit the floor. Robert stared at it for a moment and then walked to the front office, too upset to speak.

When the secretary asked him what happened, he told her the name of the boy who had knocked over the AV cart. Then he clammed up and wouldn't say another word. The secretary sat him down and told him not to move an inch. She called the school employees' union representative and explained what had happened. The rep showed up fifteen minutes later, talked to Robert quietly for

— Chapter 10 —

a few minutes, and then talked to the principal, the vice principal, and the head of HR.

Apparently, the secretary and the vice principal were familiar with this boy and his bullying, and he was already on the brink of expulsion. Robert had been an exemplary employee, so they believed him. Robert never found out what happened to the boy; he guessed it was none of his business. The school assured him that he would never have to deal with him again, and not to worry about the broken equipment. Still, Robert was done. He never wanted to see the inside of that high school again, so he quit. He felt like a failure, but he was unwavering in his decision.

A couple of years later, after taking courses in television repair at the city college, Robert landed his dream job as a TV repairman, a job he held for forty years. Quitting his first job was the right thing to do, and opened the door for so much more.

MESSAGES FROM AUTISTIC MENTORS

"I Googled how to quit a job. I give notice and then keep going to work for two weeks after giving notice, even though I'd rather leave immediately."

— Helena, works with autistic children

"When you quit, you don't get unemployment. I once reached a point where I needed to move on from a job. I wrote a thank-you

Working While Autistic

note to my employer for the opportunity and for trusting me. I also reached out to thank three coworkers who really supported me."

— Suzanne, drive-through window greeter

"One thing I've learned about myself is that I push myself hard. I try, try, try to stick with it until it's obvious that it's not going to get any better. When you get to that point, ask for a meeting, say this isn't working out for me, and give your notice. If you need to say why, then say why, but keep it professional. It helps to have a script prepared going into the meeting."

— Beth F. Watzke, late-diagnosed autistic writer and animal care provider

CHAPTER 11
Side Hustles

"Writing is a side hustle that had previously enabled me to pay for rehab for my brother, purchase a car for my parents, and help friends out when they fell on hard times."

— *Stacey Abrams*

Whether you lost a job through downsizing, quit a job that was not a good fit, or are still looking for your first entry-level position, you may find yourself unemployed. Or maybe you have a job, but it doesn't bring in enough money. You might have a passion you want to pursue, which may become more financially rewarding in the future, but it's too soon to quit your day job. You are not alone. Most adults have been where you are right now, unemployed or under-employed, in need of a second income to make ends meet in difficult times. For whatever reason, you may find that a side hustle is right for you.

A side hustle is a second job or additional income stream, usually alongside your primary job. It allows you to bring in more money while you maintain your regular employment. For some, a

Working While Autistic

side hustle is necessary to pay the bills; for others, it's a labor of love, a chance to follow a passion and see where it leads.

There are all kinds of side hustles. Some are active, like making and selling art or providing a service people need. Others are passive, like creating a course that doesn't require a lot of work once it's online. Whatever your interests, talents, and experience, the perfect side hustle may present itself. If it's something you love to do in your spare time anyway, then monetizing it is a bonus. However, beware of "get rich quick" schemes and scams on the internet. Nobody actually wins buckets of money playing games on their phone. If something sounds too good to be true, it's probably not legit.

Here are some tips to bear in mind when you start up a side hustle. We'll use the word HUSTLE to remember: *habits, understand, start smart, tell the world, learn to earn,* and *economics.*

HUSTLE

Habits

The H in HUSTLE stands for *habits*.

Before you start your side hustle, establish the habits that will support you and your success. You want to add a second job without burning out, so put your self-care first. Plan self-care activities into your daily schedule, and write them in ink, not pencil. If you throw yourself into your side hustle without established habits to take care of your own needs, your health may suffer. Remember you

Chapter 11

need to rest, stay hydrated, exercise, and eat to support your health. Balance time spent recharging your batteries with time spent at work or with social activities. Once you know that self-care is a habitual part of your daily routine, there is less risk of burnout when you add a side hustle to your daily schedule.

Other positive habits to establish include time management and money management, both critical to balancing your side hustle with your main job and your personal and family life. Make use of calendar and financial planning apps and tools so that you can see where your time and money are spent, with no surprises. (Find tips in the chapters about time management and money management in *Independent Living While Autistic: Your Roadmap to Success*.)

Understand

The U in HUSTLE stands for *understand*.

The first thing you'll need to understand before you begin your side hustle is the market. Is there a market for the product or service you want to provide? You can find out what people search for online on a trend-tracking website such as Google Trends. Type in the product you want to make or the service you want to offer, and you can see how many people have searched for that. If no one wants what you want to sell, now is the time to pivot, before you invest a lot of time and money on your side hustle. Make a slight turn or modify your product a bit; it can make a big difference. For example, there may not be much of a market for hand-knitted scarves, but you might find your audience if you sell scarves in colors associated with particular superheroes, favorite cartoon characters, or sports teams. The more data you gather about what people want to buy, the easier it will be to find your market. Be careful not to use a copyrighted word, name, or phrase in your advertising; keep it recognizable, but legally distinct from the original.

Start Smart

The S in HUSTLE stands for *start smart*.

Before you create your website or sell your first product or service, start smart and lay the groundwork for success through research and data gathering. Once you understand the market for your side hustle, find out all you can about how to start a small business in your state. You may or may not need a formal business plan to start your entrepreneurial journey. Check out the legal requirements on your state government's website under "Small Businesses." There, you can learn what the license or registration requirements are for the kind of business you want to pursue for your side hustle. It's smart to make sure you're operating legally before you go forward.

Tell the World

The T in HUSTLE stands for *tell the world*.

If you don't get the word out, no one will know about your products or services. You can't sit back and wait for the world to beat a path to your door; go out and find your people. Follow other similar artists or entrepreneurs on social media, and join groups dedicated to the interest related to your side hustle. Chances are

– Chapter 11 –

you can't afford to spend a lot of money to advertise at the beginning of your entrepreneurial journey. That's why you started this side hustle, to bring in money, not to spend it all before you've earned it. Instead of paid advertising, consider organic marketing. Organic marketing means using free marketing strategies to improve your online visibility rather than paid advertising. You can go a long way in reaching your audience with social media, blogs, a website, and a newsletter that target people who are interested in what you have to offer. When you publish content across social media channels you naturally improve your website's search engine optimization, or SEO. Start with organic SEO rather than paid advertising. It can save you a lot of money that you might not want to spend in the early days.

Your side hustle is nothing to be ashamed of, so don't hide it. Blow your own horn. You might worry that if the word gets out, your regular employer will disapprove. Of course, if you signed a contract that you would not undertake any other job in your free time, then you need to renegotiate that contract before you go forward. If your service is similar to what your employer offers, it could put you in competition with them, which would be a conflict of interest. If that's the case, you should find a different side hustle as long as you continue to work for your current employer. Other than that, you shouldn't need to hide your side hustle from your regular employer as long as you operate responsibly and ethically. This means you do not use your employer's computer, phone, internet, or office supplies for your side hustle, and you don't work on your side hustle during the hours you are meant to work on your primary job. Don't try to sell your product to your colleagues over lunch. Keep the two worlds separate. If you don't cross the line or take advantage of your employer, they should have no problem with your side hustle after your regular workday is over. You're not obligated to tell them about your side hustle, since your free time is your own, but you shouldn't feel that you must hide it either.

If you want your side hustle to grow, learn all you can about marketing, and then go out and tell the world so everyone can reap the benefits of what you have to offer.

Learn

The L in HUSTLE stands for *learn to earn*.

There is a lot to learn when you start a side hustle, and you are the perfect person to educate yourself. Start with your state government resources for small businesses. They have more to offer than you might imagine, and at no cost. Once you educate yourself through online searches, you'll find marketing books, free blog posts and websites, free or reasonably priced courses, and other resources online, so learn all you can. Follow podcasts, YouTube channels, and blogs of entrepreneurs who have successfully grown their side hustles to become financially viable. Warning: don't be fooled by anyone who says they got rich overnight, and you can, too, if you buy their course. Paying them for their "secrets to success" will not make you a millionaire overnight. Most of those are cons or scams. Lots of podcasts and bloggers offer free resources so you don't have to pay to learn while you learn to earn.

– Chapter 11 –

Economics

The E in HUSTLE stands for *economics*.

There is a lot to consider about the economic side of your side hustle. Will you need to purchase art supplies to make products you will sell? If you will mail products to your customers, make sure that the shipping/handling fee you charge fully covers the cost of mailing it, including your time. Do you need a website, email address, or post office box? You probably will. Many of these things can be managed on a small budget, but plan your budget in advance to manage the economics of your side hustle. Open a checking account for your side hustle, to keep your income streams separate and transparent. Pay close attention to the money that comes in and goes out, so you know at each step of the way whether you're losing money or making money. It's not unusual for a new hustle to start slowly, and you might see more money going out than coming in at first. That should turn a corner once you are established. Keep a close eye on your profits and losses so you'll know if you need to increase marketing or pivot and change your hustle. If economics is not your strength, seek professional wisdom, but don't ignore the topic. Economics will be the key to your side hustle's success.

As you go forward with your plan, give yourself the grace to allow your side hustle to unfold naturally. Don't expect it to pay all your bills overnight. If you make a mistake or have a setback, be as forgiving and gracious toward yourself as you would be toward someone you care about. One of my favorite quotes is by Maya Angelou: "Do the best you can until you know better. Then when you know better, do better." Whenever you start something new like a side hustle, be kind to yourself while you learn the ropes. You can't know everything all at once, but you can learn from your own and others' mistakes and avoid making them again and again. And when you know more, you will do better.

Read on for the side hustles that our six characters pursued.

SIX CHARACTERS IN SEARCH OF EMPLOYMENT

DAISY

DAISY: I can't believe it! It worked!

MOM: What worked?

DAISY: I just made twenty dollars! Twenty actual dollars, in my account, that wasn't there yesterday. I'm rich!

MOM: Well, I guess you're twenty dollars richer. Where did it come from?

DAISY: Well, you know how I'm always reading and watching videos about D&D?

MOM: Yes, I believe you mentioned D&D once or twice.

– Chapter 11 –

NARRATOR: *Sarcasm alert. The matriarch means that our hero has mentioned it multiple times, not once or twice.*

DAISY: Whatever. So, I created an online course to teach newbies the vocabulary of the dungeons, and survival tips. And someone bought it! For twenty dollars!

MOM: Can you do that, legally?

DAISY: Don't worry, I'm not using any copyrighted stuff, only what's in the SRD.

MOM: I do not know what that is.

DAISY: *(sighs)* SRD is a system reference document. It's licensed under an open game license, a public copyright license, so people don't steal the D&D stuff. I'm not about to do anything shady, Mom. I'm chaotic good, not neutral or evil.

MOM: I'm glad to hear that. But how did you do it?

DAISY: I made myself a free website, and I created a course using another free site, an online course builder. And I shared about it on the social media sites where the D&Ders hang out. And now I have twenty dollars I didn't have before!

MOM: You put a lot of work into this, didn't you?

Working While Autistic

DAISY: A ton! But it's paying off!

MOM: Have you put any time into working on your senior project for school?

NARRATOR: *The dreaded senior project! Our hero had completely forgotten it in her passion for course building ... she is doomed!*

DAISY: Uh oh. I kind of forgot about it. Are you going to yell at me? Because you're kind of slaughtering my joy right now.

MOM: Actually, I wondered if this course could be your senior project. You've already worked so hard on it, and you've proven it can generate revenue. Why don't you ask your senior advisor about it?

DAISY: Mom, that is actually an excellent idea!

MOM: You don't need to sound so surprised.

DAISY: *(hugs her mom)* Thanks, Mom! I'll go email my advisor right now.

NARRATOR: *Great joy filled the halls when our hero received official approval to use her course as her senior project. She anticipated many more sales and new courses to come.*

— Chapter 11 —

ZACH

When Zach married Crystal, he moved out of the temple basement apartment and into her small condominium. He had to give up the temple caretaker job when he moved out, which put a small dent even in their combined incomes, as his job at the assisted living facility was low paying and had fluctuating hours. He needed something else to help make ends meet; he needed a side hustle.

After some online research, Zach decided to become a delivery driver. He had saved up and bought a reliable car that was only a few years old. He kept it clean and in good repair, and he enjoyed driving, so he was ready.

There were two kinds of driving that he signed up for: driving people and delivering food and groceries. His favorite was shopping for groceries because he could use the self-checkout and minimize social interactions. He liked to pick up restaurant orders and drive through fast-food places, too. His least favorite was driving people, but since he lived in a city with an airport, he got a lot of calls. Fortunately, plenty of people requested a "quiet ride," so they didn't expect small talk. If they did want to chat, he found that if he asked them a question, like where they were headed or what kind of business they were in, he could put his attention back on the road and let them talk about themselves. People seemed to like that.

For Zach, delivering and driving were the perfect side hustles. Anytime he and Crystal needed a bit more money for an unexpected expense, he'd just open his schedule for more trips. He set his own hours, and that was something he appreciated.

Working While Autistic

TRISH

Trish put the finishing touches on the alumni newsletter, *The Wall*, before she sent it off to the printer. It was named after an old brick wall, only about a yard long and a couple of feet high, perched inexplicably in the middle of the main lawn on campus. It had been a landmark of the college for as long as anyone could remember. The Wall was famous for its changing colors and messages. Overnight, different societies, clubs, or groups would sneak out and paint The Wall in their colors or splash their messages across it. During football season and during pledge week The Wall changed just about every night. Students might wake up to find it sporting a top hat, or with beer cans glued to the sides, even neon feathers. The Wall was such a fixture it was no wonder their alumni newsletter was named for it. Trish still loved to check out The Wall every day when she came to work, and she loved writing and publishing *The Wall Alumni Newsletter* as part of her job.

One day she got an email from one of the alumni representatives, complimenting her on what a good job she always did with the newsletter. Trish felt her face grow warm in embarrassment, but she was pleased that the work she did mattered to others. She never even knew if anyone read the newsletter or not. The email went on to ask her to produce a newsletter for their graduating class, which would go out monthly for the year leading up to their big reunion. They wanted to make sure everyone knew what was going on, who would be attending, and when they needed to confirm their reservations.

— Chapter 11 —

Trish asked her supervisor, Stacie, if it would be appropriate for her to take this on and showed her the email.

"I'm afraid we can't authorize you to do this as part of your workload here, Trish," Stacie said. "You have enough on your plate as it is."

"Oh, okay, I'll tell her no, then." Trish was a little disappointed, as it had sounded like fun.

"Wait a minute, she offered to pay you. You could take it on as a side hustle, outside of your work hours."

"Would that be okay?" Trish didn't want to overstep.

"As long as you do this from home, on your own time, using your own computer and whatever else you need, it's fine. I think they'd really appreciate it if you could do this for them. Plus, every young family could use a little extra income sometimes, right?"

"Right, thank you, Stacie." Trish was excited to accept the offer. Since this would be an e-newsletter, there were no materials needed and no printing or mailing. She had the programs she would need on her home computer, and it wouldn't take too long. She could work on this during the evenings when Bill was busy on his computer and little Jimmy (now too old to be called Baby James) was sleeping.

The reunion committee was so pleased with her work, they shared her contact information with other alumni representatives. Soon, Trish found herself with a regular side hustle that she enjoyed, producing newsletters for alumni groups and societies.

Working While Autistic

BILL

Bill had always been a devoted builder of LEGO® bricks. It was not a childhood interest to be outgrown, but a lifelong passion.

Perhaps it was this love of building that inspired his side hustle as a furniture assembler. There was a large IKEA® store in their city, and Bill and Trish enjoyed shopping there, especially during less busy times of the day. They loved the Swedish meatballs, and their first home was furnished straight out of the IKEA® catalog. As soon as they got a new piece home, Bill couldn't wait to start the build. It was like LEGO® for adults. He couldn't figure out why so many people struggled to assemble their furniture; it was easy for him. His furniture assembly side hustle started with a family member who asked for his help, then another, and soon word got around. He went online to see what people charged for in-home furniture assembly. To his surprise, he learned that his local IKEA® was partnered with a handyman company that hired people for various tasks, including assembling furniture. He created an email account for "Bill the Builder" and used it when he signed up for the handyman service. It wasn't long before he started getting jobs. He printed business cards that said, "Bill the Builder, quiet furniture assembly. I work better and faster when people don't chat with me while I work. Thank you." When he arrived for a job, he handed the owner the card, and they usually left him alone to do the work he excelled at and enjoyed. It was the perfect side hustle for a LEGO® lover like Bill.

– Chapter 11 –

MARIA

Maria loved putting together intricate models of giant transforming robots. She also enjoyed YouTube videos of other people putting together their models. Sometimes she found it annoying though. Some people made mistakes in their construction but left the mistakes in the video so the audience could see where they went wrong. Other people chatted on and on about nonsense the whole time they put their model together. Maria did not enjoy either type: the imperfect assemblies or the running commentary. Why didn't someone just make a video that showed the correct way to put the model together without talking about it?

When her daughters, Faith and Hope, were home from college on a break, she complained to them about how frustrating it was that no one seemed able to make a serious, correct, and quiet video of constructing giant robot models. They said she should do it herself. Maria didn't think that sort of thing was her cup of tea at all, but the twins got busy. They rigged up a holder for her cell phone around her neck so that the camera was pointed toward her table, not her face. They found some classical music that was free to download and use in Reels. Finally, they told her that if she put her next model together while wearing her camera, they would edit it and add music and subtitles describing the model and where to buy it. It turned out to be a lot of fun for all of them and gave Maria an excuse to keep on buying model kits. When the girls shared the link on social media groups for robot fans and model builders, she started getting a lot of likes and followers. Eventually, the channel had one thousand subscribers and averaged four thousand watch hours for a year. At that point it started making money. Not a lot, but enough for a bit of extra pocket money.

In the meantime, Maria continued to take on temp work doing proofreading for small publishers. She put up a notice at the local university to help grad students proofread their theses and dissertations, which increased her income somewhat. Between her temp work, helping students with proofreading, and her YouTube channel, she was able to make ends meet without worrying too much about money. It was a comfort.

ROBERT

"Dad, have you ever thought about being a parent advocate?" Lena sat in the chair across from Robert's recliner in the family room.

"Apparent what now?" Robert put down his newspaper and looked at his daughter over the tops of his reading glasses. To be honest, he put down his electronic tablet on which he was reading the news, since the women in the household had decided that actual newspapers were old-fashioned and bad for the environment.

"Parent advocate. Someone who goes with a parent to their child's IEP meeting. They make sure that the school district follows the rules and doesn't take advantage of parents who don't know their rights."

"Well, I've been to every one of Bobby's IEP meetings, and I never saw them break any rules or stomp on his rights."

"We have a great school district. But some parents feel anxious in IEP meetings. It can be overwhelming, and they want someone

— Chapter 11 —

in their corner, someone who understands special education law and will speak up for them if they aren't comfortable speaking up for themselves and their child."

"I guess that makes sense. But why are you telling me this stuff?"

"Well, a couple of my friends in the parent support group want to hire a parent advocate informally."

"Informally?" Robert still didn't see where his daughter was going with this.

"They don't want to hire an expensive lawyer if there's no need for that, but they do want an advocate to sit by them at the IEP table. They'd feel better if they had someone with them, informally." Lena smiled. "I think they want to scare their school district a little bit."

"Scare them? But the schools and the parents are on the same team. Everybody wants what's best for their kid. Why make it all adversarial?"

"And that's exactly why you'd be perfect for the job. You respect the school's position, but you've also always kept the focus on what's best for Bobby."

"Well, as I recall, I wasn't always so welcome at Bobby's IEPs." Robert smiled ruefully.

"True, the first time you attended with me, you asked so many questions that we had to extend the meeting to another day. But you learned."

"I guess I'm not too old to learn a thing or two. But I still don't know why you're telling me about all this parent advocate stuff."

Working While Autistic

"Well, my friend AnneMarie wants an advocate to sit with her on the three-year IEP re-evaluation meeting for her son, Elliot. And I think you'd be perfect."

"Honey, if your friend wants to borrow a grandpa for Elliot, of course, I'm happy to go to the IEP with them. Elliot and Bobby are such good friends, we're like family."

"Thanks, Dad, but she wants to pay you for your time to attend the meeting. Not as much as she'd pay a lawyer, but something. She says she won't feel right about it otherwise."

Robert frowned. "I don't need the money, we do okay, but if she really wants to pay, we can put it in Bobby's future fund. You know, for college or whatever he needs. You and AnneMarie can work out the finances, just tell me when and where to show up."

"Thanks, Dad! This means so much!" She gave her dad a hug before she headed back to the kitchen to help her mother with supper.

Robert harrumphed quietly, shook out his tablet slightly as if shaking out the pages of a newspaper, and went back to scrolling the news. He wasn't looking for a side hustle, but if he could help another family just by showing up for their meeting, then why not? He chuckled softly, thinking he could hang out a shingle, "Grandpa for Hire."

— Chapter 11 —

MESSAGES FROM AUTISTIC MENTORS

"I have tried a few side hustles while I was a stay-at-home mom. There was a lot to keep track of, and it made me feel scattered and anxious. I think finding your boundaries and your priorities is important."

— Helena, works with autistic children

"I have two side hustles. I'm a crafter making personalized crafts to sell, and I'm also a life coach with a podcast, *The Aspie Bridge*. For me, what works best is to work my main, bill-paying job at the beginning of the day rather than taking a closing shift. It's easy to get emotionally involved in the side hustle, so you might get carried away and be late to work, or forget to go, or be too tired to work your regular job."

— Suzanne, drive-through window greeter, crafter, and life coach

"The college where I was teaching writing went through changes, and I began losing classes, so I got into animal daycare on the side. I segued into becoming a pet care provider, and I also continue to write."

— Beth F. Watzke, late-diagnosed autistic writer and animal care provider

— PART IV —
Retirement and Beyond!

"I found out retirement means playing golf ... But to me, retirement means doing what you have fun doing."
— *Dick Van Dyke* —

– CHAPTER 12 –
Retirement Planning

"Smart financial planning—such as budgeting, saving for emergencies, and preparing for retirement—can help households enjoy better lives while weathering financial shocks."

— *Ben Bernanke, economist*

You may think you're far too young to think about retirement, but if you're today years old, it's time. You will probably live a long life, and chances are you won't want to work full-time forever. Everyone deserves to rest from their life's labor in their golden years, and that includes you. It's stressful to worry about whether or not you can meet your basic needs. You may not need riches to have a happy life, but you want to be able to buy your groceries with the same confidence at the end of the month as you did at the beginning of the month. Your comfortable future won't happen overnight though. It takes a lot of advance planning to secure a carefree retirement.

In addition to retirement income, medical insurance will be important. If you were fortunate enough to have health benefits in your job before retirement, they will not automatically continue after retirement. Make an appointment to talk with the person at your business who handles benefits and find out if you're eligible for COBRA (Consolidated Omnibus Budget Reconciliation Act) or the Affordable Care Act. Learn what is possible and what makes sense for your situation. Also be sure to research what is available through Medicare or Medicaid.

Medicare is a federal program that can begin as early as age sixty-two, or earlier in the case of disabilities covered by Social Security. Find out if your autism diagnosis makes you eligible for disability services. Medicare includes Part A for hospital coverage and Part B for doctor fees and lab fees. Part C may be provided through private insurers, and Part D covers prescriptions. This is a very brief summary to give you a general idea; you should consult your Social Security office to find out what is available for you and how to access it.

Medicaid is also a federal program, but it is administered by the states. It's available for low-income people regardless of their age. It covers basic health care needs like doctor visits and hospital stays, but it can also cover eyeglasses and nursing home care. Research what Medicaid services are available in your state and how to sign up for them.

In addition to finding the post-retirement health coverage that's right for you, start early to learn all you can about what retirement options are available for you. How do you plan for retirement? There are a number of things to consider.

Use the word SILVER to remember these: *social security, investments, learn, verify, employer matching, Roth.*

— Chapter 12 —

SILVER

Social Security

The S in SILVER stands for *social security*.

The Social Security Act has been around since 1935. It was designed to pay retired workers a continuing income after retirement by having the government collect it and save it for them. Workers put money into social security when their employers deduct it from their paychecks. At retirement, they get paid monthly from social security. The amount they receive is based on how many years they worked at jobs that deducted social security. Some jobs don't deduct social security. Students and young workers who babysit or do yardwork do not have any of their money withdrawn and deposited into social security. If you work in the public sector, such as a school district, you will pay into a government pension plan instead of social security. Most jobs do deduct social security, and when it's time for you to start withdrawing it at retirement, know that this is your money, not a handout. You pay for it with every paycheck deduction, and you deserve to enjoy it when you retire.

Investments

The I in SILVER stands for *investments*.

Not everyone can afford to invest in things like the stock market. If you have some extra money and you want to earn more interest than a simple savings account, especially if you won't need to withdraw it soon, then investments might be right for you. If you go this route, be sure to consult with someone knowledgeable and trustworthy and learn all you can before you give them your hard-earned nest egg to invest.

Learn

The L in SILVER stands for *learn*.

Whether your retirement includes social security, investments, a pension plan, or other funding sources, learn all you can in advance. There are many free courses and podcasts about financial matters. The more you learn about your retirement options, the more confident you'll be about the decisions you make.

Verify

The V in SILVER stands for *verify*.

Not everyone who claims to be a financial advisor with your best interests at heart is who they say they are. Be smart about who you believe so you don't get fooled by a charismatic speaker who promises get-rich-quick schemes. There are sites online that have information about whether something is a scam or legit. Read reviews by others who have used their financial services. Don't rely on the reviews they put on their own websites, which will all be positive, but check the internet for criticisms too. Verify that the financial advisors you want to trust are as trustworthy as they seem.

Employer Matching

The E in SILVER stands for *employer matching*.

Some employers will match funds in a retirement plan. This is a great option, and you would be smart to take advantage of

— Chapter 12 —

it. Employer matching is an easy way to earn twice as much in retirement savings as you would have done on your own.

Roth

The R in SILVER stands for *Roth*.

A Roth IRA is an individual retirement account where you may contribute after-tax dollars. This means your money can grow tax-free. Once your account has been open for at least five years and you are older than 59½ years old, you may withdraw your money tax-free with no penalty. It was named after Senator William Roth who, with Senator Bob Packwood, led the creation of the retirement plan in 1998. They wanted to restore the traditional IRA in which contributions were not tax-deductible and which had been repealed in 1986. The new Roth IRA would let Americans have a plan with an upfront tax deduction.

Let's read on to learn how each of our fictional characters dealt with retirement issues.

SIX CHARACTERS IN SEARCH OF EMPLOYMENT

DAISY

Daisy graduated from high school and earned an AA degree in business and communication. Lilac hired her full-time at Lilacs & Lattes once she graduated, and she became a valuable team member, and eventually a manager. She continued to create and

Working While Autistic

sell courses and later e-books related to D&D-type role-playing games.

You can read in *Independent Living While Autistic* how Daisy found a local D&D game where she could join others rather than just watching games on the internet. She met and befriended Crow, a nonbinary fellow D&Der with purple hair and many piercings and tattoos. The story of how Daisy and Crow fell in love and became an official couple is in *Relating While Autistic*. Their little family grew unexpectedly in *Parenting While Autistic* to include not only their faithful dog, Bugbear, but also Kitty, a transgender teenage girl who needed a home.

When her mother decided to join her best friend in a retirement village, she signed over to Daisy ownership of the quadruplex home Daisy had grown up in. It was small, but it was paid for, and the familiar four walls gave Daisy comfort. As her family grew to include Crow, Bugbear, and Kitty, there was always room for all. Coziness was something she treasured.

Because her needs were simple and she didn't go overboard on spending, Daisy had been able to save a little bit of money every payday. Her dream was to buy her own coffee shop/nursery someday. Unfortunately, she was never able to save very much. Every time she had a good amount in savings, something came up: a dental crown, a plumbing issue, car repair. It was always something. It looked like her dream of owning her own place was not in the cards. When Lilac was ready to retire, she asked Daisy if she wanted to buy Lilacs & Lattes from her. There was no way Daisy could come up with a down payment, so she had to pass. Then

— **Chapter 12** —

Lilac offered to lease it to her until it made her enough money to buy it. That was the perfect solution! Once Kitty graduated from college, Daisy hired her to work in the shop. Kitty learned the ropes quickly and was soon managing everything. Daisy started to think about retiring herself.

> DAISY: So, I've been thinking about retiring.
>
> CROW: Really? You love working with Kitty. I'm surprised you'd want to retire.
>
> DAISY: Well, you said you were retiring next year, so I thought I'd retire, too, so we could spend more time together.
>
> CROW: It would be fun to travel, with Kitty holding down the fort here. We've never really been anywhere, have we?
>
> DAISY: I've always been so much more comfortable with everything always the same, no changes, but I think I might be ready to try something new.
>
> CROW: How about Wales?
>
> DAISY: What about whales?
>
> CROW: Would you like to visit? They do have a dragon on their flag ...

Working While Autistic

NARRATOR: *Whales don't have flags, with or without dragons. Stop and evaluate before responding. What are we missing? Who has a flag with a dragon?*

DAISY: Wales? Sure, I'd love to visit Wales! As soon as I finalize my retirement plan.

CROW: What do you mean, finalize it? We've been putting a bit of money aside since we got married. It's not much, but it's better than if we hadn't been saving all along. Anyway, we'll both be eligible for social security soon.

DAISY: I know, but I have a way to make our money go even farther! It's a new investment opportunity where we can earn 500 percent on the dollar!

CROW: That does not sound real. Where did you hear about this? And did you give them any information or money yet?

DAISY: Well, not yet. I wanted to wait until I told you about it to get started, of course. It sounds like a great deal, though, that we can't afford to pass up. Here, I'll forward you the email I got so you can see how amazing it is!

CROW: *(reads email)* I don't think this is legit, Daisy. Let's verify it online. I'll do a search with the company's name and the word "hoax" and see

— Chapter 12 —

CROW: *(continued)* what we come up with. *(taps on their phone, then shows Daisy the screen)*

DAISY: Ohhh ...

NARRATOR: *Our hero has narrowly missed being swindled by a retirement hoax targeting the elderly. Thank goodness for Crow's suspicious mind.*

CROW: I'm sorry, Daisy.

DAISY: I guess it did sound too good to be true.

CROW: Yeah. But we have enough to take a trip to Wales, if we travel economy and mind our pounds and pence.

DAISY: Pound a fence?

NARRATOR: *Sometimes Crow made no sense at all.*

CROW: Pounds and pence, dollars and cents. We just have to pinch our pennies, no splurging, and no falling for online scammers.

DAISY: That could have been disastrous if you hadn't verified it and found out the truth.

CROW: Your optimistic and trusting nature is one of the many things I love about you, chaotic good dwarf of my heart. Unfortunately, there are evil people out there who would take advantage.

Working While Autistic

DAISY: I guess you're right. Anyway, let's forget all that and plan our trip to Wales!

CROW: Good idea.

DAISY: By the way, can we also go whale watching sometime? No reason, unrelated, the idea just came to me ...

ZACH

As he approached his sixties, Zach felt like he had a lot to learn about retirement. Crystal's job included a pension. Zach knew he had put into social security in his job at the assisted living facility where he'd worked for so long. At one point he had to reduce his hours because of autistic burnout. As he aged, he found that the level of physical effort required to lift and support patients to transition them from bed to wheelchair was too much for him. Fortunately, he was able to take a sideways "promotion" to a desk job where he completed paperwork for several workers who handled the heavy lifting. His side hustle of driving and delivering was something he continued to enjoy, and it was easy to increase his availability whenever they needed extra money. However, he wondered if he had made a mistake in not sticking with full-time work.

Fortunately, Zach discovered when he started researching retirement, all the money he'd paid into the required self-employment tax for driving and delivery had gone into social security for him. They weren't rich, and they would have to be careful with

— Chapter 12 —

their money, but he was better prepared for retirement than he had feared.

TRISH & BILL

Trish's and Bill's jobs and side hustles were not stressful, but they knew some day they'd want to retire. Fortunately, retirement for them would not mean a decrease in income. Trish's employer, the college she'd loved as a student and throughout her career, provided a retirement plan with employer matching, and she'd been putting money into it faithfully since her first paycheck. Bill had been paying into social security all along, but in addition to that he'd made a few smart investments. One was with a company whose products he already used, a store that sold video games. He bought a few shares, then a few more. It was exciting to see the numbers go up and his little nest egg increase, but after a while he took his money out and put it into a stable, interest-earning savings account. Some people stayed with it and made loads more money, but Trish and Bill didn't need to be wealthy. They were happy with their simple life, knowing they could afford to retire whenever they were ready. They even had enough savings to treat Jim and his family to a vacation with them every summer. It was a wonderful life, and Trish's employer-matching retirement fund along with Bill's social security and investments had made it all possible.

MARIA

Maria was apprehensive about turning sixty, but not because the milestone birthday meant she was old. She'd always seemed older

Working While Autistic

than she was, and she accepted it. She worried that she might not have enough money to live on as she got older. She could still manage the temp work and dissertation-editing jobs, and her side hustle of making YouTube videos of constructing model robot kits supplied her with a bit of money. A tiny bit, but not zero. But what about the future? Most of her adult life, she had been a stay-at-home mom, so she hadn't contributed to social security for those years.

When her daughters visited her with their families for Easter, they noticed that she seemed more tense. They could see it in her increased hand fluttering and the way she pressed her fingers into her cheeks when she was stressed. After the family Easter egg hunt in the back yard, the twins got their husbands and children settled in front of the TV to eat candy and watch Easter cartoon specials. Then the girls sat Maria down at the kitchen table with a cup of tea and asked her what was wrong.

She admitted that she was worried about the future, that she might not have enough money for retirement. Faith and Hope assured her that they would always be there for her, and they promised to look into retirement for her.

A few weeks later they joined her on a group video call to tell her what they learned. Because she had been married to their dad for more than ten years, she was entitled to social security after she reached retirement age, based on his work history. Also, while she worked at the publishing company, she paid into social security for herself. They also learned that her temp agency had withheld social security along with taxes, so she continued to contribute

— Chapter 12 —

to her future retirement. It wasn't a lot, and she would still have to be careful with her spending, but she wouldn't starve. Not that her daughters would let that happen, but Maria found it nearly impossible to ask for help, no matter how much she might need it.

Maria was so relieved! Still, she thought she should deposit money regularly into her savings account in addition to social security. Before she started making YouTube videos of constructing robot models, she used to buy one or two model kits every month. As she gained viewers, the model kit companies sent her free kits in exchange for promoting their products on her channel. She decided to take the money she would have spent on kits and put it into her savings account at the beginning of every month. It wasn't a lot, but it would add up. Maybe as her small income from the videos grew, she would put away even more money into savings. What would happen when her old house needed a new roof? She didn't want to have nothing saved up for a rainy day, especially if that rainy day meant filling her house with pots and pans to catch the rain dripping from her ceiling. In any case, knowing that there would be social security for her when she reached retirement age was a huge weight off her mind.

ROBERT

Robert hadn't stayed at his first job with the school district long enough to get vested into their retirement plan. Fortunately, his next job as a TV repairman lasted over thirty years. Not only did he pay into social security all those years, but the company had a Roth IRA program that he'd signed up for. He and Helen still

Working While Autistic

lived in the same house they bought when they got married, and it was paid off. Between social security and his Roth IRA, they didn't really need the small income he got from his part-time job in the fixit shop or his side hustle as a parent advocate. It felt good not to have to worry about money and to enjoy their golden years.

MESSAGES FROM AUTISTIC MENTORS

"I have a 401K, and I added a divorce settlement to it. My advice is to always keep an emergency amount of money in an account. Put aside a little bit of money as you go."

— Suzanne, drive-through window greeter, crafter, and life coach

"I feel like I can't retire. I'm afraid social security won't be enough to live on, so I'll keep working and looking for jobs I can still do as I get older. They didn't used to teach us about finances when I was in school. I'd like to continue to work with animals and connect with other people and write. Keep on working if you love what you do, and if you can, give back to the community and be useful. You can be an asset in retirement."

— Beth F. Watzke, late-diagnosed autistic writer and animal care provider

— Chapter 12 —

"Even though I'm not near retirement age yet, I save for retirement. It's really important. I feel lucky to have enough income to save some, and I like to save and plan for the future."

— Helena, works with autistic children

— CHAPTER 13 —
The Adventure Continues ...

"Life is either a great adventure, or nothing."

— *Helen Keller*

SIX CHARACTERS LIVE AND WORK HAPPILY EVER AFTER

DAISY

Daisy and Crow did take their trip to Wales, and coincidentally, they also went whale watching, unrelated. Lilacs & Lattes grew and became more profitable under Kitty's management, and now they have both indoor and outdoor café seating. Most mornings, you will find Daisy and Crow enjoying the flowers and sunshine, Daisy with her pumpkin-spice latte and Crow with their peppermint mocha. Bugbear the Third usually naps nearby in a sunny spot or laps up a whipped cream treat that he invariably gets all over his furry face. All of the regulars know them, and many stop by and visit. Daisy knows all of their dogs' names and personalities, and Crow knows the humans' names. They still play D&D every week, but now they hold the game at Lilacs & Lattes after closing. Kitty makes sure everyone has their favorite snacks and beverages.

On this night, our hero, Daisy, waits for the twenty-sided die she rolled to land. As it bounces from one side to another, Daisy realizes it doesn't matter what number comes up. She could roll a twenty, or she could roll a one. It really doesn't matter. Daisy has had the luckiest and happiest life she could have wished for, with her beloved Crow, their daughter Kitty, and faithful Bugbear the Third, all together. No roll of the dice could improve on that.

ZACH

When Zach's parents were in their late seventies, they announced their plans to move into an assisted living community. They'd already done all of their own research, and they knew what they wanted, so they handed Zach their car keys, called the movers, and that was that. Zach was relieved that he wouldn't have to make the call and tell them they were too old to drive or live independently. They had taken all of the responsibility themselves, knowing that making important decisions could be stressful for their son.

Zach visited them several times a week for the rest of their lives, so he was familiar with the facility. It was clean, with lots of windows letting in sunshine, and a garden area where residents could enjoy the out-of-doors. Their small apartment had a mini-kitchenette with a microwave and mini-fridge. They could choose to eat in the dining room, have their meals delivered to

— Chapter 13 —

their apartment, or fix something for themselves, whatever they preferred.

When the time came that it was difficult for Zach and Crystal to take care of their home, rather than burdening their own children, it seemed natural for them to choose the same retirement community for themselves. For Zach, familiarity was important. It was hard for him to adjust to new things, and this would be an easier move than if they had made a different choice. Crystal knew this about her husband, and she was with him 100 percent. Their kids and grandchildren lived close enough to visit sometimes, which was nice.

Zach enjoyed watching Crystal play card games or put together jigsaw puzzles and chat with a group of ladies. It was so easy for her to make friends, and everyone loved her. Zach would sit and listen to podcasts or audiobooks and watch her smile and laugh from across the room. It made him happy to know that when he died, she would have a strong support system already in place. Statistically speaking, he knew that women tended to live longer than their husbands, and he hoped this would be true for them. As he looked back over his life, he realized that marrying Crystal and the family they raised together was far more important than any job he'd held. Work was important, sure, but the people you loved made life sweet.

TRISH & BILL

Trish and Bill had a long, happy marriage. They loved each other, they loved their jobs, and they loved their son, Jim. Now that their

Working While Autistic

boy had a career and family of his own, they were empty nesters. They settled into a comfortable life not unlike what they had shared as newlyweds before Baby James came along.

For a while after they retired from their primary jobs, they continued with their side hustles and put away the extra money into savings. Over time, it became more difficult for Bill to put in the physical effort required to assemble furniture. Trish lost interest in her side hustle e-newsletters after she'd been away from the college for a few years. Eventually, they retired from these side jobs as well and enjoyed a quiet retirement.

They had been bringing in a young person to do heavy housework once a month, and over time, they increased her hours to every Monday, and in addition to housework, she prepared simple meals they could microwave easily. Then, one day, she showed up on a Wednesday. She told them that their son, Jim, had hired her to come in three days a week for the rest of the year, and then it would be five days a week after that.

They called him to protest that it was too much, but he was firm in his decision. He said that whenever he asked them what they wanted for Christmas or their birthdays they never wanted anything, so this would be his gift to them. It allowed them to remain in the sweet familiarity of their own home as they grew old together. Trish and Bill thanked him and said they couldn't imagine a better gift. They agreed that they must have done something right raising him.

– Chapter 13 –

MARIA

Faith and Hope and their husbands bought a duplex near Maria's home. It was such a joy to see her grandchildren regularly, but for short periods of time, since she tired more easily as the years went by. It was lovely to see them arrive, so excited to tell their grandma all about their activities and interests, but it was also good when their moms took them home after an hour or two.

Both of her daughters did regular meal prepping for their own families and put together a week's worth of lunches and suppers every weekend. They got together every Saturday and chatted and caught up while they chopped vegetables and assembled casseroles. They always included lunches and single suppers for Maria and brought them over every Sunday for the next week.

Maria hadn't realized how tiring it had been for her, not only the cooking, but planning and deciding what to make. Her world was so much simpler when all she had to do was open her refrigerator and read the sticky note on the container on top of the stack. She hoped her girls weren't sacrificing their own time and happiness to take care of her, but they seemed to truly enjoy their sister time in the kitchen each Saturday while their husbands enjoyed active play and trips to the park with the kids.

Maria hoped she would never have to move out of this home where she had raised Faith and Hope; it was filled to the brim with happy memories and the comfort of the familiar. With the help of her girls, it looked like this dream could come true for her.

Working While Autistic

ROBERT

Robert and Helen made a will and left their home, which was paid off, to their grandson Bobby to inherit. They knew he struggled with employment himself as a young autistic man, and they wanted to make sure he would always have a roof over his head, as long as he paid the taxes on the property.

One Sunday after a family supper, Bobby asked his grandparents if he could move back into his old room. After he had completed his AA and had a job as an entry-level IT specialist, he had been proud to move into his own studio apartment. However, times were hard, and sometimes he struggled to pay all of his bills. Also, he hoped that he would be able to help his grandparents as they got older. They had helped him and his mom for his whole life, and he wanted to return the favor.

After some discussion, it was decided that Bobby would be their live-in support person. He would keep his IT job, but he'd work from home, so he'd always be close if needed. Robert realized that if he ever fell down, Helen would not be strong enough to help get him back on his feet. Not that he was about to fall down; he wasn't that old yet, not by a long shot! Still, it would be hubris to assume it couldn't happen. Now that Robert and Helen were getting on in years, having Bobby live with them again was a happy, companionable solution.

– Chapter 13 –

MESSAGES FROM AUTISTIC MENTORS

"After almost fifty years in health care, I had to let go of it and retire. My advice is, don't let anyone make you think you're 'abnormal.' There's a lot of strength and value that comes with being on the autism spectrum. Just keep looking for yours."

— Jane, retired medical professional, late-diagnosed autist

"I've found so much acceptance and support in the neurodiversity-positive community. Reach out to the community and make connections with other autists. You are not alone. Learn more about yourself and how your autism expresses, because we are all unique. Stay positive, stay connected, and find safety and belonging in the ND community. There is support for you. There is joy."

— Beth F. Watzke, late-diagnosed autistic writer and animal care provider

GETTING IN THE LAST WORD

As I write this last chapter in what I believe will be the final book in the *Adulting While Autistic* series, I look back over my own work life. After college and grad school, I was a special education teacher for the better part of twenty years, with a few years spent as the principal of a small Quaker school. I went back to school to

Working While Autistic

become a school psychologist, and for the next twenty years, that was my career, including ten years exclusively assessing toddlers to determine eligibility for autism services. As a lifelong learner, as I know many of you are, too, I continued my education to become a licensed educational psychologist and then earned a religious studies doctorate in pastoral counseling with a specialization in counseling related to autism. I became an adjunct instructor and enjoyed a "side hustle" of teaching in university graduate programs for school psychologists in the evenings after my day job was finished.

I retired from my career in public education in 2016. When I realized that retirement wasn't my cup of tea, I became an author, speaker, and CEO founder of Adult Autism Assessment and Services. How long will I continue to work on these post-retirement careers? Who knows? I know that I love what I do, so I will probably go on for the foreseeable future.

What about you? Do you love what you do? If so, congratulations! I hope that your career of choice brings you joy and financial support in full and equal measure. You deserve that.

What if you don't love what you do? It may be time to re-evaluate your career path. What aspect of your work life is not working for you? Are there things that could be changed for the better with the right accommodations? If you're happy enough with your job but it doesn't bring in enough money, can you see a path forward to a promotion and raise? It may mean going back to school to get additional training, or it may be as simple as asking your supervisor about opportunities for advancement. You could

— Chapter 13 —

leave this job for a better-paying one if you're not thrilled with it, although I would suggest you wait until you have your next job secured before you quit. Or perhaps a side hustle, separate from your day job, is what you need to be in a better place.

Wherever you are on your personal adventure of working while autistic, assess your strengths and abilities along with your needs and accommodations, and evaluate the market and the possibilities. This is a good way to know which way you should proceed. Planning is key, from your first job search and interview, every step of the way until retirement. It's not always easy, but you can do hard things. That's what it says on the sticker on my water bottle, "You can do hard things," and I believe it.

Trust yourself. Prioritize self-care. Take a deep breath and step out into your future.

You've got this!

"Strive not to be a success, but to be of value."
— *Albert Einstein*

"It is neither wealth nor splendor, but tranquility and occupation which give you happiness."
— *Thomas Jefferson*

IN GRATITUDE

There are so many people who have contributed to this book, and I am deeply indebted to them and grateful for their help, encouragement, and support.

- The amazing team at Future Horizons, especially Jennifer Gilpin Yacio, Susan Thompson, and Karen South.

- My writing family and dear friends Cherie Walters, Cynthia Whitcomb, Diane Hagood, Kristi Negri, Laura Whitcomb, Linda Leslie, Pamela Smith Hill, and Susan Fletcher.

- My first reader, Cynthia Whitcomb; collaborative reader Siobhan Marsh; and sensitivity readers Cat David Marsh and Noel Marsh.

- My inspiring siblings, authors all: Jonathan Whitcomb, Cynthia Whitcome, Laura Whitcomb; and the memory of our parents, David Whitcomb and Susanne Wise Whitcomb, who always encouraged us to follow our hearts.

- My children, who have had my back throughout this post-retirement writing career: Cat David Robinson Marsh, Siobhan Eleanor Wise Marsh, Noel Maebh Whitcomb Marsh; and always near us in spirit, their father, my beloved David Scott Marsh.

Working While Autistic

- Finally, and importantly, the autistic mentors who so graciously shared their own employment journeys, insights, and advice: Beth F. Watzke, Helena, Jane, Noel, Scott, and Suzanne. Because of you, this book will be so much more meaningful and helpful than it could have been otherwise. Your authentic voices are vitally important, and I am grateful to you.

RESOURCES

Ambitious About Autism. "Starting a New Job When You're on the Spectrum." https://www.ambitiousaboutautism.org.uk/about-us/media-centre/blog/starting-new-job-when-youre-spectrum.

Baker, Jed. *Preparing for Life: The Complete Guide for Transitioning to Adulthood for Those with Autism and Aspergers Syndrome.* Arlington, TX: Future Horizons, 2005.

Cook, Sarah Teresa. "For the Birds." Substack. https://sarahcook.substack.com.

Craft, Samantha "35 Interview Tips for Those on the Spectrum" on *The Art of Autism* https://the-art-of-autism.com/35-interview-tips-for-those-on-the-spectrum/

Grandin, Temple and Kate Duffy. *Developing Talents: Careers for Individuals with Autism*, third edition. Arlington, TX: Future Horizons, 2024.

Jyoti, Christine Ryan of LearnVest "7 Secrets for a Successful Side Gig." on *The Muse.* https://www.themuse.com/advice/7-secrets-for-a-successful-side-gig.

Mantell, Mike "Office Politics: The Do's, Don'ts, and Absolute No-Nos." on *Science of People.* https://www.scienceofpeople.com/office-politics/.

Marsh, Wendela Whitcomb. *Independent Living While Autistic: Your Roadmap to Success.* Arlington, TX: Future Horizons, rev. 2024.

Pantelakis, Alesandros. "What Is Work Ethic, and Why Is It Important for Success?" on *Workable: Resources for Employers* https://resources.workable.com/hr-terms/what-is-work-ethic.

Price, Devon. *Laziness Does Not Exist.* New York, NY: Atria Books, 2021.

Price, Devon. *Unmasking Autism: Discovering the New Faces of Neurodiversity.* New York, NY: Harmony, 2022.

Sanok, Joe. *Thursday is the New Friday: How to Work Fewer Hours, Make More Money, and Spend Time Doing What You Want.* New York, NY: HarperCollins Leadership, 2021.

Working While Autistic

Ward-Sinclair, James "Finding Jobs for Autistic People: A Complete Guide to Autism and Employment." on *Autistic & Unapologetic*. https://autisticandunapologetic.com/2021/03/15/finding-jobs-for-autistic-people-a-complete-guide-to-autism-and-employment/#first-steps/.

Wylie, Philip. *Very Late Diagnosis of Asperger Syndrome (Autism Spectrum Disorder) How Seeking a Diagnosis in Adulthood Can Change Your Life*. London and Philadelphia: Jessica Kingsley Publisher, 2014.

Author Bio

Wendela Whitcomb Marsh, MA, RSD, is an award-winning author, TEDx Speaker, and founder of Adult Autism Assessment & Services, a nation-wide neurodiversity-affirming group practice. Her books include *Recognizing Autism in Women and Girls* and *Homeschooling, Autism Style*, among others. *Working While Autistic* is the fifth book in her Adulting While Autistic series. Learn more about her books at https://www.WendelaWhitcombMarsh.com and about the group practice she founded at https://www.AdultAutism Assessment.com.

Praise for *Recognizing Autism in Women and Girls*
"In the last ten years, we have become increasingly able to identify how autism may be expressed differently in girls and women. This new comprehensive and engaging resource (*Recognizing Autism in Women and Girls*) outlines those differences and may encourage parents and autistic adults to seek a diagnostic assessment, which should, in turn, improve the diagnostic abilities of clinicians. The lives of so many girls and women will be transformed by recognising their autism."
— Tony Atwood, PhD
Psychologist, Professor, Author, International Speaker

Praise for *Parenting While Autistic*
"*Parenting While Autistic* is chock full of information on autistic considerations through all ages and stages of parenting from initial planning, pregnancy and birth all the way through each stage of a

Working While Autistic

child's growing up, including leaving the nest. Regardless of which stage of parenting you may find yourself, if you are an autistic parent (or planning to become one), you will want to read this book! Besides the valuable information, each stage of growing up is accompanied by several types of family stories that allow the reader to see how the information presented is implemented in a variety of family configurations and situations. This makes it easy for the reader to imagine forward in their own family, planning implementation of strategies for successful parenting while autistic. Quite valuable!

    — Judy Endow, MSW, LCSW
        Author, International Presenter, Mental Health Therapist, Autistic Parent and Grandparent

Did you like this book?

Rate it and share your opinion!

BARNES & NOBLE
BOOKSELLERS
www.bn.com

amazon.com

Not what you expected? Tell us!

Most negative reviews occur when the book did not reach expectation. Did the description build any expectations that were not met? Let us know how we can do better.

Please drop us a line at info@fhautism.com.
Thank you so much for your support!

FUTURE HORIZONS

www.ingramcontent.com/pod-product-compliance
Lightning Source LLC
Jackson TN
JSHW020839280425
83386JS00001B/1